HATTIE COTTON SCHOOL

HATTIE COTTON SCHOOL

The last teacher's first-hand experiences of the 1957 bombing and aftermath…

STEPHEN MACKENZIE

PREMIUM PRESS AMERICA
NASHVILLE, TENNESSEE

HATTIE COTTON SCHOOL
By Stephen MacKenzie

© 2024 Stephen MacKenzie

Published by PREMIUM PRESS AMERICA, Nashville, Tennessee

ISBN: 978-1-933725-85-7
Library of Congress Catalog Card Number: 2024901003

PREMIUM PRESS AMERICA books are available at special discounts for branding, premiums, sales promotions, fundraising, or educational use. For details contact The Publisher at
6581 Jocelyn Hollow Road, Nashville, TN 37205-3950;
or phone 615-353-7902, or fax 615-353-7905.

To contact The Author, write or call The Publisher.

Text and cover design by Phyllis Rose, 828 Marketing,
phyllis@828marketing.com

All photos have been provided by the
"Special Collections Division, Nashville Public Library."

Printed in the United States of America
10 9 8 7 6 5 4 3 2 1

"Not everything that is faced
can be changed,
but nothing can be changed
until it is faced."

—James Baldwin

Dedication

This book is dedicated to my amazing wife of over forty-five years, MaryAnne MacKenzie. Her story, from all those years ago, inspired me to write this book. She has been my major source of information, my first proofreader, my sounding board, and my biggest cheerleader. This has been an unbelievable adventure— and I could never have done it without her.

It is also dedicated to the memory of
Patricia Watson and Margaret Cate.

Preface

It was a warm June morning in 2018, late morning actually, when my wife MaryAnne and I took a ride out to East Nashville, Tennessee to see the Hattie Cotton School, where she had taught sixth grade back in the 1950s, long before we met. We had been visiting her hometown of Nashville at least once annually since we married in 1978, and we had talked about going out to Hattie Cotton for years, ever since we had started talking about writing this book; we'd just never found the time. As Robert Frost penned, *"way [had always led] on to way,"*[1] and we'd just never gotten there. But this day the timing worked. After several years of thoughtful planning, this book was finally going to become a reality.

We had spent several hours over two different days earlier in the week at the Nashville Public Library, researching. We discovered a plethora of information on the desegregation process within the Nashville School District, along with a number of accounts of the bombing of the Hattie Cotton School and its aftermath. *The Nashville Tennessean* and *The Nashville Banner* both published numerous articles about the shocking event. *Life* magazine published a feature article including a cover photo of the school's principal, Miss Margaret Cate. In 2007, honoring the fiftieth anniversary of integration in the Nashville elementary schools, Alexander Street published a film documentary titled *A Child Shall Lead Them,* which featured several of the children and their parents who made the walk that broke the barrier of segregation.[2] And in its September 2018 edition, *The Nashville Retrospect* headlined the Hattie Cotton bombing. We were also fortunate enough, while at the library, to actually bump into Tennessee author Betsy Phillips, who was researching a number of bombings throughout the South during the civil rights period. She offered to share any of her research with us, since we were not working on competing projects, and she did in fact provide us with several FBI files which proved to be very useful in documenting the bombing and immediate aftermath.

---

[1] Robert Frost. "The Road Not Taken."
[2] A Child Shall Lead Them

Taking up an entire table in the Special Collections room, we requisitioned files and folders, one after the other, dozens of them. We read each one thoroughly, took notes, and made copies—lots and lots of copies. We searched through photos, letters, official documents, and what seemed like miles of microfiche. But what we did not find during our research, were any books written about the Hattie Cotton bombing. I cannot categorically state no such books exists, but I can say we were unable to find one.

As we headed east up W. Greenwood Avenue this June morning, the light blue sky was filled with white fluffy clouds. The sun was warm but not oppressive, as it can be this time of year in Tennessee. Before long the school was in sight and we slowed down, pulling our small, white rental car to the side of the road in front of an older but well-maintained bungalow style home. I stepped out of the car to take some pictures and shoot a short video. What we were photographing was the Hattie Cotton STEM Magnate Elementary School, a modern looking red brick, two-story building with a green-roofed tower in the middle. Between the street where we were parked and the school itself was a divided parking lot, split with a strip of bright green lawn, and landscaped with several varieties of shrubs near the building. Larger trees sprawled around the parking area.

A few minutes later we pulled into the driveway and parked. Getting out of the car the warmth contrasted significantly with the coolness of the compact Chevy's air conditioning. We heard birds and crickets singing along with cicadas and katydids chirping. A series of strokes and persistent neuropathy had slowed MaryAnne down, but they hadn't stopped her, and we slowly made our way from the parking lot to the front door. Once inside we were fortunate enough to be greeted by the administrative assistant.

Before leaving we also met the current principal, Ms. Jocelyn Adams. A very pleasant and welcoming Ms. Adams informed us she had recently been appointed to the principal's position at Hattie Cotton. We chatted for several minutes about the school today, how it had changed in late years, and how much she loved her job as its head administrator.

MaryAnne told her she had been a teacher at Hattie Cotton in 1957, the year desegregation had begun in Nashville. She went on to say that hers had been one of the four classrooms which were significantly damaged by dynamite following the first day of school, and her class was displaced for the next several months. We talked for a few minutes about our plans to write a book, and our desire to hold the initial launch of it right there at Hattie Cotton, which pleased her greatly. We also mentioned that, with her permission, we would like to design some sort of memorial of the bombing as our gift to the school, something which did not currently exist. She loved the idea.

MaryAnne is the last living faculty member from that fateful school year. For her, coming back to East Nashville was like going through an old photo album found in the bottom of a trunk tucked under the eaves in the attic. The building and the people were far different from when she had worked there. But the neighborhood—the houses and streets—all had a look of vague familiarity.

I walked around several of the neighborhood streets and knocked on some doors. I thought it might be worth a shot to see if anyone still lived in this diverse area who had been there in 1957. I chatted briefly with an elderly black woman sitting on her front porch. She said she remembered the bombing but couldn't recall any details. A white man who might have been in his mid-sixties or so, actually seemed to get a bit defensive regarding my rather benign questions. He asked, "Just what is it you're trying to accomplish with this anyway?" I spoke with a couple of other people but gathered no additional information. Still, it was poignant, walking streets which had been part of MaryAnne's life long before I was, thinking about a time that had been so significant for her, and so painful.

As we were leaving to go back to our hotel, we took one more slow drive around the school building, and MaryAnne reflected on the visit. She was thrilled to see the school, its new look, its beauty, and to know it was still educating children. Driving back along W. Greenwood Avenue. MaryAnne took note of the area where she had stood with her colleagues looking at the school that fateful September morning back in 1957, a time when it looked very different.

It would be two-and-a-half more years (Robert Frost again), plus a life-disrupting global pandemic, before I would get down to serious work on writing the book. But here it is, April of 2021. I am working at the computer in our winter home in Puerto Plata, Dominican Republic, trying to pull it all together. Some days are a bit of a struggle, like today, as I look out the window in front of my desk. In 85-degree sunshine, the clusters of magenta and peach colored bougainvillea waving in the breeze, backed by a blue and cloudless sky, are urging me to join them. But this story needs finishing, MaryAnne continues to proofread and encourage, and my deadline approaches. Today, MaryAnne and my deadline are going to win.

Introduction

For years it had been one of our go-to stories, one of those defining moments you really can't tell or hear too many times—like you just can't quite get enough of it. You know it's true while you're hearing it but you just can't hardly believe it. "Honey, tell me the story of Hattie Cotton again. Tell me about Margaret Cate walking that little girl out to her car to take her home. What was the girl's name? Take me through your bombed out classroom again when you first stepped into it." Time and time again I asked for it to be repeated. It had all the scenes of a historical drama, the heroes of an epic poem, the *beyond-belief* details of a work of fiction or fantasy, and the mayhem of a horror story. But my wife's account of her first year as a teacher at Hattie Cotton Elementary is definitely tragic nonfiction.

All the exact details of how and when I heard MaryAnne's story the very first time, I can't recall, and they're not important anyway. What is important is the story itself, the impact it had on her and her students at the time, and the impact it made on me several decades later. I think she was gently taking me to task for some racist joke I had told, or comment I'd made. Forty or so years of life-experience later, I am ashamed to even think about, never mind admit to, some of the things I have said in my past, some of the jokes I've told. Today, I would sooner drop dead than make a racist comment or tell a "black joke," but back in the day…like so many of my peers, in a lot of ways I was an insensitive and unthinking idiot.

When I think back on some of my racist behavior as a kid—even as a young man—I cringe. The foolish things I said I didn't even believe; I said them because my friends did. I laughed because they did. I don't recall us ever using the "N" word, because even white idiots, most of us anyway, had a sense that it crossed the line. But don't think that stopped us from telling the latest joke making the rounds in white circles, jokes about porch monkeys or limousines with "darkies" to drive them, or diets of fried chicken and watermelon. Today, when I think about my friends who are black, people I look up to, respect, love…I feel such horrible guilt I cry on the inside…sometimes even on the outside. Right now, when I think about some of the people I love sitting down to read this book—family members, life-long friends, former students, people who have always shown me such admiration and respect—I cannot tell you how incredibly ashamed and embarrassed I am. Insensitive, oblivious, ignorant—just plain stupid. It's why when I ask my students to write about something for which they feel at least a little twinge of shame, those are the things which come to my mind. It's why I struggle even to sing old hymn lyrics like "wash me and I will be whiter than snow."[3] It's why when politicians ask if we should be paying reparations, I usually think, *better we should be down on our knees begging forgiveness.*

Is it "white guilt," a term which is tossed around a lot these days? I don't know, but I do know when I think of some of the cruel things I've said, even if I didn't mean them, I do feel guilty. I don't feel guilty for being white; I feel guilty for my behavior. Is the guilt I feel the result of "white privilege?" Again, I don't exactly know. I do know this, as middle-class-average as my economic and social standing has always been, I have had untold advantages in my life because of two things, two things into which I made no contribution whatsoever, not one thing to do with my skills, my abilities, my brains (or lack thereof), absolutely nothing: where I was born and the color of my skin. So, you know what? If I feel some "white guilt" because of my "white privileges," too bad for me, because I probably should.

Anyway, responding to MaryAnne's brief reprimand about the dehumanizing effects of racism, I recall saying something like, "Honey, no offense, but you're white. You grew up in a state where slavery was once the law of the land, and you've lived in overwhelmingly white New Hampshire for something close to thirty years. Remember the time when we were visiting your family and I was reading aloud from an article in The Tennessean about classes at Tennessee State? It was your aunt who said, 'Huh, I wouldn't walk across nigger town to get there.' Seriously, what do you know about how blacks feel? What makes you an authority on the effects of racism?" She stayed quiet for several seconds, with a slightly hurt look in her eyes. I don't know what I expected to receive for an answer, probably some quick barb or witty retort, but whatever I expected, it wasn't what I got.

---

[3] Whiter Than Snow, Nicholson, Fischer

What slowly rolled out was a story unlike any of the other better-known stories of the Civil Rights era. It had nothing to do with Rosa Parks or the bus boycott in Montgomery, Alabama, or the riots and protests in Little Rock, Arkansas, nothing to do with the Rev. Dr. Martin Luther King Jr. or the March on Washington, nothing to do with anything I had ever read or learned about in history or social studies classes. I had studied King's *I Have a Dream* speech. I had seen documentaries on Rosa Parks, and I had learned about Emmet Till. I knew several New England ministers in my denomination, including the pastor of my Methodist church in Dover, NH, had been among the thousands who marched on Washington, D.C. No, this was a story about a small, neighborhood elementary school in East Nashville, Tennessee, a school for first through sixth graders, shattered by hatred and rebuilt by the strength and will of a determined principal, the dedication of a committed staff, and the indomitable spirit of a community.

At the center of the story was my MaryAnne, who in September of 1957 was a second-year teacher, beginning her first year at the Hattie Cotton Elementary School. The Hattie Cotton story probably did more to define and chart the course of MaryAnne's career than any other single event she ever experienced during her fifty-plus years in education. Her outstanding colleagues at Hattie Cotton helped drive her to earn a Master's degree in education. Remembering the needs of her 1957 students helped inspire her to return to the classroom for her Certificate of Advanced Graduate Studies in counseling. And the example of Margaret Cate was there when she decided to pursue doctoral studies in administration.

So moved was I by the Hattie Cotton story that it was a strong influence on my own decision to change careers and enter the field of education. Some forty years later that fateful night helped define the kind of teacher I would become. Like MaryAnne, I often use literature to help teach some larger, more universal lesson. Also like her, I find myself highly sensitive to issues of race and prejudice. Perhaps the most important thing MaryAnne taught me, based on her experiences from 1957, was to love my students—always and no matter what.

Make no mistake, though, this story is not about me. I may be doing the writing, but this is the story of a horrific event as seen through the eyes of MaryAnne, the last living faculty member from 1957. Through formal interviews, informal chats, and substantial research I have tried hard to capture the essence of that horrible night and its aftermath: the hate, the love, and the hope. So yes, this is MaryAnne's story, but in a very real way these pages also tell the story of Margaret Cate, Irene Spivy, Patricia Watson and many others. I hope I have done them all justice.

"We conclude that in the field of public education the doctrine of "separate but equal" has no place. Separate educational facilities are inherently unequal. Therefore, we hold that the plaintiffs and others similarly situated for whom the actions have been brought are, by reason of the segregation complained of, deprived of the equal protection of the laws guaranteed by the Fourteenth Amendment."

— Brown v. Board of Education (1954)

PART ONE
(The Back Story)

We can never be satisfied as long as our children are
stripped of their self-hood and robbed of
their dignity by signs stating: *'For Whites Only.'*

—Rev. Dr. Martin Luther King, Jr.

Chapter One

While we can trace America's racist roots to its earliest recorded history, established in large part by southern plantation owners' ever-expanding quest for cheap labor, shamefully, the doctrine of separate but equal was born in the courtroom of the nation's highest and most powerful legal body: the United States Supreme Court. Long before there were public busses, where Rosa Parks would be arrested and fined, kindling a city-wide boycott, there were passenger trains, where Homer Plessy would be arrested and fined, kindling a famous and precedent-setting lawsuit. In 1887, Florida had been the first state to pass legislation requiring rail companies to provide separate cars for black and white passengers. Other southern states quickly followed Florida's lead, one of them being Louisiana. In 1892 a group of black passengers decided to challenge the Louisiana law using Homer A. Plessy as the lead plaintiff.

Plessy v. Ferguson went all the way to the U.S. Supreme Court and in 1896 the court issued its decision. It declared that a law which "implies merely a legal distinction" between white people and people of color did not violate the Fourteenth Amendment and therefore was not unconstitutional. Separate, they claimed, did not mean inferior. In fact, with only one dissenting vote, that of former slaveholder Justice John Harlan,[4] the 1896 Supreme Court decision effectively allowed that segregation of the races was constitutional in virtually all public settings. The justices based the ruling on their differentiation between "civil rights," which are protected constitutionally, and "social rights," which are not. So, while Homer Plessy had a protected civil right to vote, for example, he did not have a protected social right to sit where he wanted on a train.

On the strength of the Supreme Court's decision that separation of public facilities by race alone was not unconstitutional, so long as the

---

[4] History.com Editors. "Plessy v. Ferguson."

separate facilities were equal, state legislatures quickly began to enact what came to be known as the Jim Crow laws. Signs went up across the south: White Only train cars, White Only seating areas in restaurants, White Only sections in theaters, courthouses, and churches, White Only public restrooms. These conditions were not only socially acceptable, with whites of course, now they were legal. The racial divides set up by *Plessy v. Ferguson* multiplied rapidly. The "merely legal distinction" was observed in nearly every public facility throughout the United States. Separate but Equal was born. It would define public policy and control the interaction between whites and blacks in America until the middle of the twentieth century.

As incredible and impossible as it must have seemed, the 1896 Supreme Court decided Homer Plessy and another eight and a half million American blacks could not sit in a train where they wanted. They couldn't watch a movie or a play where they wanted. They couldn't eat in a restaurant, go to school, nor worship God where they wanted. This entire group of American citizens, millions of them, couldn't even urinate where they wanted. Yet, all of these together, according to the Supreme Court, the ultimate arbiter of American justice, did not violate the 14th Amendment, which guarantees all United States citizens equal protection under the law. Sadly, one is almost left wondering just what was gained in 1865. Not only did *Plessy* fail to achieve its objectives, striking down the laws of racial segregation, but the court's decision affirmed and upheld them, essentially allowing—no, encouraging—them to become systemic. It is not even a reach to suggest, while the Emancipation Proclamation clearly dismantled institutional slavery in America, *Plessy v. Ferguson* just as clearly laid the foundation for institutional racism. As a result, over the next half-century *Plessy's* "separate but equal" was not just the law of the land in these "United" States, it would become a way of life.

Chapter Two

The 1950s were a period of great social change in American society. The United States had emerged from World War II as the world's only major superpower. The economy was expanding rapidly. The baby boomers were filling maternity wards. Manufacturing output was on the increase. Personal income was rising. Home ownership was setting new records. It was a great time to be an American, at least if you happened to be a white, Anglo-Saxon, Protestant American, and preferably a male. Of course, if you didn't happen to be white, things probably weren't quite so good for you, and it likely wasn't such a great time to be an American.

The decade of American dominance and prosperity was also the decade which revealed black Americans lagging behind white Americans in virtually all sectors of the nation's economy: Household income, savings, higher education, employment, homeownership. Segregation was at its peak throughout U.S. society. In short, if you were white, you were probably part of the American Dream. If you were black, you were probably dreaming about being part of America.

It is difficult to imagine the kinds of racial tension which existed in the pre-civil rights era. Most U.S. citizens today can't imagine any American having to sit or not sit in certain seats on busses or in designated cars on trains. We can't conceive the norm of *Whites Only* bathrooms, restaurants, and drinking fountains. And we certainly can't imagine laws not only allowing but requiring racially segregated public schools. Yet, until the latter part of the 1950s, "White" schools or "Colored" schools were exactly what we had in the United States.

It was 1952 when America elected World War II hero and Supreme Allied Commander in Europe, General Dwight D. Eisenhower, as its thirty-sixth president. Whether it was his upbringing or his first-hand knowledge of the horrific results of policies put in place by the racist and anti-Semitic regime of Adolf Hitler and his Nazis, Eisenhower understood America could not remain a racially divided nation. The period of Reconstruction being an exception, for nearly a century following their "freeing," black Americans had endured forced, legal separation from whites in most public facilities, particularly throughout the South. They were tired of their second-class status, segregated bathrooms, and designated seating areas. More and

3

more, black citizens, along with growing numbers of their white neighbors, were recognizing these conditions had to stop. As Lincoln knew a united America could no longer survive slavery, Eisenhower knew America could no longer survive *separate but equal*. It defied morality and defiled our very founding creed: *E Pluribus Unum*. In sending a gift to America, a statue which would become the world-wide symbol of freedom, and to which would be added the inscription "Give me your tired, your poor, / Your huddled masses yearning to breathe free…"[5] the French people must have frequently wondered what on earth they had been thinking. Thankfully, many Americans saw the duplicity as well, including the president.

For all of Eisenhower's military and political accomplishments, the appointment of the moderate Earl Warren in 1953 (and the even more progressive James F. Brennan in 1956) to the U.S. Supreme Court, thus shaping the nation's highest legal body for the next two decades, may have been his greatest service to the country he loved. During Eisenhower's second term the Court would make profound, precedent setting changes in American Constitutional law. It is clear, as history shows, Eisenhower would have preferred slower, more gradual change, speeds less prone to significant controversy, action, and reaction. It is equally clear, however, he could foresee the potential consequences of his appointments—and he made them anyway.[6]

Eisenhower did not attain the status of general, nor the office of president, by shying away from responsibility or controversy. He was a leader, a successful one, and those leadership skills would be tested here in America as they had been in Europe and elsewhere. By the mid-fifties, reacting to the Supreme Court's ruling, anti-integration demonstrations were occurring all across the South. In order to uphold the US Constitution, amid much criticism from both segregationists and integrationists, Eisenhower took the risk of sending Federal troops into Little Rock, Arkansas to safeguard the nine black students who were attempting to integrate all-white Central High School. Governor Faubus, who had defied the Supreme Court order, discovered just how formidable

---

[5] "The New Colossus."
[6] Kahn. "Shattering the Myth."

the president's leadership skills were.[7] Finally, America would have to begin building a bridge—and one day fully cross it—if it had any hope of ever becoming what it so hypocritically pledged to be: One nation, under God, with liberty and justice for all.[8]

[7] Eisenhower and the Little Rock Crisis
[8] Pledge of Allegiance

Chapter Three

In 1951 litigation began which would make it all the way to the US Supreme Court. Something had to be done regarding the disparities in public education. While there had been a few challenges to the Jim Crow laws between the 1896 *Plessy v. Ferguson* decision and the civil rights movement of the mid-twentieth century, they were largely unsuccessful. For more than fifty years *Plessy* and its *separate but equal* laws and practices stood firm. So Oliver Brown, along with several other black families, filed suit against the board of education in Topeka, Kansas, where Brown's daughter had been denied entrance to the school nearest their home. Citing *Plessy v. Ferguson,* and noting that in Topeka, the separate facilities were indeed fairly equal, the court ruled against the plaintiffs. Brown *et al,* then turned to the US Supreme Court, which agreed to hear their appeal. Represented by the lead attorney for the NAACP and future Supreme Court Justice Thurgood Marshall, *Brown v. the Board of Education* would live to fight another day.

The outcome at the federal level, however, was anything but guaranteed, for in 1952, when the Supreme Court agreed to hear *Brown v. Board of Education*, the Court was still headed by Truman appointee Chief Justice Fred M. Vinson. Some historians have asserted the court was divided on the issue of school desegregation, speculating several of the justices believed the court lacked the authority to mandate integration, presumably seeing it as a states' rights issue. It is possible, they argue, a Vinson court might have let *Plessy* stand. But then, in September of 1953, Vinson died of a heart attack. By the time the case was actually heard by the high court, Eisenhower's appointee, Earl Warren,[9] had replaced Vinson as chief justice.

Despite the equalities evidently existing in the Topeka schools, Marshall and his team were able to demonstrate clearly and convincingly

---

[9] History.com Editors. "Brown v. Board of Education."

that in general all-black schools were not equal to all-white schools, in fact black schools lacked in nearly every measurable area. White schools were much better funded. They had "better buildings and equipment, newer textbooks, higher levels of teacher training, smaller pupil-teacher ratios, closer administrative and school board oversight."[10] So, armed with fifty-eight years of 20-20 hindsight, hundreds of hours of testimony, reams of affidavits and transcripts, along with a huge dose of social conscience, human awareness, and moral responsibility, the Warren Court considered everything Brown *et al* had to offer and everything the Board of Education used to refute. And while the Court listened and deliberated, the nation impatiently awaited its decision.

---

[10] Egerton

Chapter Four

Fully recognizing the gravity of their landmark decision and the precedents it set in *Brown v. Board of Education,* the United States Supreme Court, on May 17, 1954, changed the course of American history. With the guidance of Chief Justice Warren, the Court's nine judges unanimously voted to overturn *Plessy* and declare legally enforced, compulsory segregation of the nation's public schools did in fact violate the equal rights protections for African Americans guaranteed under the Fourteenth Amendment. It also violated, according to the Court, the right to due process provided by the Fifth Amendment. *Plessy v. Ferguson* had to go: "separate" *did,* in their judgement, mean inferior. Public schools across America would have to be desegregated.

Unfortunately, in a land built on the notions, beliefs, and laws that blacks were not actually human beings, were inferior to whites, and were in fact meant to be "owned" by whites, the Supreme Court's unanimous decision was not met with unanimous agreement. It was not long before the resistance began to organize, and the courtroom drama spilled into the streets of many cities across the nation. Desegregation, no matter how legally and morally correct, would not come easily or quickly.

Opposition to the Supreme Court's decision in general, and to integration in particular, came from many places and struck from many angles. All across the South, groups like the Klan, and other white supremacist organizations banded together in an effort to kill desegregation. In the state of Tennessee, the Tennessee Federation for Constitutional Government (TFCG), arguably "the state's foremost massive resistance group during the 1950s,"[11] and the White Citizens Council were the chief opponents to integration. The latter was little more than a band of street thugs, while the former "spoke to a sort of mannered segregationist attitude in Nashville and elsewhere trying to subvert the racial change promised by the *Brown v. Board of Education* decision to broader racially conservative principles."[12]

---

[11] "We Kept the Discussion at an Adult Level"
[12] Ibid.

They attacked the Supreme Court decision, the justices themselves, the US District Courts, the state boards of education and local school boards. They attacked local, state, and national politicians, the National Association for the Advancement of Colored People (NAACP), as well as the black parents and their children who might dare to "darken" their all-white schools. Their goals were simple: Defy, defy, defy; and if that didn't work, delay, delay, delay. The segregationists were not going down without a fight—and they were fighting to win.

Chapter Five

Following the 1954 ruling, some states, Tennessee included, struggled in their efforts to comply with *Brown* because of the vagueness in some aspects of the decision. Other states used those ambiguities to look for loopholes so they could avoid complying. The fact is the Court did not mandate states or local governments to desegregate immediately. Providing no timeline or specific process for desegregation may have been intentional, an effort perhaps, to stem the probability of mass resistance. It may also have been to grant time to local governments and school boards to formulate their own plans based on local conditions and circumstances. In any event, the Court eventually ordered hearings for input from the states for how and when the *Brown* decision should be implemented.

To help provide more definitive guidance, but still trying to avoid hard and fast mandates for states to desegregate, the Court, in May of 1955, issued a follow-up ruling. *Brown II,* as it would become known, required all students in America, whether black or white, to be admitted "to public schools on a racially nondiscriminatory basis with all deliberate speed." Unfortunately, many states immediately began exploiting the latitude which "all deliberate speed" still afforded. They took the lack of specific mandates or deadlines, an obvious attempt by the Court to respect states' rights, as a license to hold out—and they did.

Virginia was especially egregious in its lack of compliance with *Brown.* One county actually closed its public schools. It then took the unprecedented step of paying tuition and sending its white students to private all-white schools, which were not subject to the federal mandate to desegregate, and to which black students could not apply. Any black children in Prince Edward County were simply on their own. They could move to another county or remain uneducated. Eventually, the US Supreme Court outlawed the practice, and Prince Edward was ordered to reopen its schools, but not until five years had passed.[13]

---

[13] "The Closing of Prince Edward County's Schools."

Arkansas also did everything it could to defy the federal mandates of *Brown I and II.* It took the showdown between Governor Orville Faubus and President Eisenhower, along with the use of Federalized Arkansas National Guard troops, before Faubus would bow to the legal and political pressure. United States soldiers had to be called out to protect black Americans from white Americans. It was like fighting part of the Civil War all over again. That is how deep the roots of segregation were in the South. That is how pervasive and systemic white supremacy was in the former Confederacy. That is how ingrained the racist attitudes were in a broad swath of the public psyche.

The Court's *Brown II* ruling left considerable leeway to the states—probably too much. Oversight was handed off to the Federal District Courts, who would have the final say in approving and signing off on the desegregation plans for every school district in the country. The process of desegregating America's public schools was challenging and far from perfect. At least, however, the process had begun. At worst the decades-long policy of *separate but equal* had been issued a death sentence, and at best a new era in the civil rights movement was born. Sadly, eight more years would pass before the Rev. Dr. Martin Luther King Jr. would passionately share his Dream with and for America. But, nearly sixty years after losing his lawsuit, Homer Plessy's dream was slowly coming to fruition.

Chapter Six

Even with the end of school segregation seemingly at hand, the resistance was strong, and dug in up to its belt buckle. In addition to those states that began enacting legislation designed to stall the integration process, or preferably kill it outright, in early 1956, most of the congressional delegations from the former southern slave states had banded together and drafted the so-called Southern Manifesto, officially the Declaration of Constitutional Principles. And it was being pushed hard. While it did not call for unlawful action, the rhetoric was harsh and directed primarily at the Supreme Court, assailing what it claimed was the illegal overreach of the judicial branch, usurping states' rights.

Key arguments of the document included the claim, "the unwarranted decision of the Supreme Court in the public-school cases is now bearing the fruit always produced when men substitute naked power for established law."[14] Presumably this "fruit" referred to the anxiety and unrest regarding the privileged "rights" of white Americans across much of the southern United States, certainly not the long over-due advancement of human "rights" for African Americans.

Perhaps the most bizarre claim of all in the Manifesto is the one which asserts, "this unwarranted exercise of power by the Court, contrary to the Constitution, is creating chaos and confusion in the states principally affected. It is destroying the amicable relations between the white and Negro races that have been created through 90 years of patient effort by the good people of both races. It has planted hatred and suspicion where there has been heretofore friendship and understanding."[15] There was definitely "chaos and confusion" between blacks and whites within the southern states. But to declare there had previously been "amicable relations" built upon "friendship and understanding" clearly demonstrates the minds of the Manifesto's writers and signatories were far more chaotic and confused

---

[14] "The Southern Manifesto," n.d.
[15] Ibid.

than the relationships to which they referred, so much so that even an attempt at rational commentary on them now seems irrational.

It is almost unfathomable that in the mid-Twentieth Century so many southern states, having rebuilt and regained tremendous prosperity in the years since the Civil War had torn the nation apart, would risk alienating themselves again from much of the rest of the country in order to maintain segregation. Yet in delegation after delegation, city after city, there it was: defy where possible, delay where not. Given the horrors which would unfold, it should be noted, ironically and remarkably, the Tennessee delegation did not sign on to the Manifesto. Still, unfathomable or not, the document had wide support among the former Confederacy. It is even more unfathomable that in 1955 there were three lynchings in the United States, the most infamous being Emmett Till. Yes, in the year when Eisenhower was pushing for the national motto "In God We Trust," right in the middle of the 1950s "Golden Age of Capitalism," two Mississippi men abducted, savagely beat beyond recognition, shot, killed, wrapped barbed wire around the neck of, and tossed in the river the fourteen-year-old Till—and got away with it. Unfathomable! But it happened.

While the South would not cede easily nor quietly, *Brown I and Brown II* were now the law of the land. Changing a century or more of thinking, literally transforming a way of life, must have seemed a nearly impossible task, even to supporters of integration, but it had to start somewhere. The integration of the nation's public schools, according to the Supreme Court, was that starting place. America had to begin equalizing civil rights for *all* its citizens, not just the ones with white skin. More than complying with the law, it was, at its core, simply the right thing to do. How sad it took several hundred years of slavery, a devastating civil war, a presidential proclamation followed by decades of continued discrimination and court battles—just to get started.

Chapter Seven

Initially, the efforts of the white supremacists appeared to be successful. More than a year after the *Brown* decisions, many southern cities, Nashville included, still had no viable plan in place to desegregate their schools. But on September 23, 1955 Alfred Z. Kelley, a Nashville barber and civil-rights activist, along with several other black families, filed suit in federal district court. Represented by Nashville attorneys Z. Alexander Looby and Avon N. Williams, Jr., and assisted by the NAACP's Thurgood Marshall, the group sought to bring Nashville into compliance with Brown.[16]

Arising from the fact Kelley's son Robert was having to commute to the all-black Pearl High School, when all-white East High School was within walking distance of his home, *Kelley v. Board of Education* is what ultimately forced the Nashville School District to develop a plan to desegregate its schools. There were, however, a few hiccups in formulating a plan which the district court would accept as meeting the "with all deliberate speed" clause in *Brown II*.

On February 20, 1957 a key paragraph of the Plan was rejected by the U.S. District Court for Middle Tennessee. It seemed the court was in no mood to acquiesce on either "deliberate" or "speed." When the initial plan was submitted to the court, it proposed integrating only the first grade at the start of the 1957/58 school year. Additionally, it proposed the Instruction Committee should "continue its study of the problem and recommend by December 31, 1957, the time of and the number of grades to be included in the next step to be taken in further abolishing compulsory segregation." The Court made it clear it would not accept the ambiguity and leeway the Board of Education wanted and insisted on a more definitive timeline and action plan. The revised plan, accepted by the Federal Court read, "that the Board of Education shall submit to the Court not later than December 31, 1957,

---

[16] Linda T. Wynn

a report setting forth a complete plan to abolish segregation in all remaining grades of the City school system, including a time schedule thereof." Originally proposed by then Tennessee Attorney General Roy Beeler in August of 1954, the Nashville School District was about to come into compliance with the Supreme Court's ruling.[17]

And so it was, in the spring of 1957, the Nashville Board of Education finally adopted what came to be known as their "stair-step" plan, which contained the detailed process by which desegregation of its schools would occur. It wasn't perfect and the implementation was slow, but it was a plan. September 9, 1957, would see the very first black children—first graders—enter previously all-white elementary schools, if they chose to do so.

[17] Egerton

Chapter Eight

In many ways, it was the best of times in America. By 1957, U.S. society was fully immersed in the American decade of Golden Capitalism, of unity, of making money, of baby boomers, of Elvis. More than a decade after the end of World War II, it was the year the first Frisbee hit the market, American Bandstand made its debut, and the now famous '57 Chevy rolled off a Detroit assembly line. It was also the year public school desegregation finally came to Nashville. Yet, in a nod to Dickens, 1957 America was also the worst of times, for it was the year of the Little Rock nine, the year the Klan forced a black truck driver, Willie Edwards, to jump off a bridge to his death, and the year of Senator Strom Thurmond's record setting filibuster against the civil rights bill. Yes, even in the face of a Supreme Court mandate, the opponents of desegregation came from everywhere. And they took their opposition and divisiveness to anyone and everyone who would give them voice.

The worst of the protestors was one Frederick John Kasper, "a well-traveled professional agitator from New Jersey,"[18] who since the mid-1950s, had been making quite a name for himself across the South. Long a vehement anti-Semite, he had begun adding white supremacist to his resume, under the guise of wanting to preserve the "purity and dignity" of *all* races.[19] And it was easy to warm up to Kasper. He was, after all, "a tall, handsome, twenty-six-year-old firebrand whose drawl and dress (white shirt and tie, tan suit with matching Texas-style hat) concealed his evolving identity."[20] Frankly, Kasper had no personal interest in the integration issue whatsoever, save an insane racist belief system he wanted to foist on everyone else—not to mention an obvious and insatiable need for attention.

[18] Egerton
[19] John Kasper
[20] Egerton

Kasper had made his first stop in Tennessee in the fall of 1956, in the small town of Clinton, where the local high school was struggling with integration. There he found all-too-willing audiences for his message, exhorting whites to press by any means necessary their defiance of desegregation. He was nearly successful in blocking the admission of black students to the high school, "but the local leadership was ready and willing to obey the law."[21] Still, because of the huge numbers of protesters and the small number of Clinton police officers, conditions were extremely dangerous. But for Governor Clement calling in dozens of state troopers and eventually hundreds of National Guard members, white supremacists might have prevented the integration of Clinton High, at least temporarily.

No matter what, though, Kasper was not without an audience and means. While in Clinton, he was arrested and bailed at numerous times, along with others of his supporters. No matter the charge he found a way to secure his release. As journalist John Egerton noted, from his arrival in mid-1956 until spring of 1958, through all the trials, testimony, and decisions surrounding desegregation, "Kasper was usually in Tennessee but only rarely in custody."[22] The man was a purveyor of racism, hatred, and violence. But he was polished, slick, and well-funded.

There were obviously those who supported Mr. Kasper, who were motivated by his fiery speeches. His presence was in great demand amongst the anti-integration crowd. There were many who might not be moved to violent demonstrations, but subscribed to his beliefs and opinions nonetheless, even reveled in them. Yet Kasper's opinions and rhetoric went far beyond trying to motivate a crowd to action. His ideas weren't just provocative, they were incendiary and seditious. His gatherings were designed not just to exercise civil disobedience, but to incite the rebellion and riots he so clearly wanted.

Is this a harsh characterization of John Kasper? Perhaps it is, but an entirely accurate one. One need not search very hard to see the huge

---

[21] Egerton
[22] Ibid.

divisions in today's twenty-first century political landscape. But even here, even when politicians often brand their opponents as misguided, accuse them of being misinformed, in certain cases they get called out as illogical or delusional, sometimes even branded extremists. Some might want to see their political opponents punished for perceived wrongdoings. Yes, they might want to see them punished, maybe censured, recalled, impeached, tried, convicted, even imprisoned—but not put to death, and certainly not murdered. In just one paragraph of a May, 1957 article, which appeared in the Virginia Spectator magazine, John Kasper stated the following about those he saw as his political opponents:

As to the Federal judiciary, we have seen continuous treason from that branch of government since Roosevelt came into power. The 9 swine on the U. S. Supreme Court, the present Attorney-General Brownell, Federal Judge Robert Taylor at Knoxville, Federal Judge Hoffman in Virginia, Federal Judge Rives of Montgomery, Alabama (race-mixing on buses infamy), and more than 75% of the present Federal judiciary should be tried for treason to the American people, for treason to the Constitution of the United States, and for attempted genocide, as this same Court once decreed in Nuremberg. Once convicted they should be "publicly hanged until dead, dead, dead," and drawn and quartered in some prominent public place (in front of the White House) to remind the public of the fate of judicial tyrants, all in the best Anglo-Saxon tradition. History shows that when despots set themselves up and flaunt the people by loving what they hate, or hating what they love, their natures become twisted and they come to a bad end, violent end, because they are acting contrary to Nature. In this struggle, wishful thinking is a decadent vice: it matters not one jot to us if these evil men ultimately meet death in a natural manner, by their own hand, or from an infuriated populace, or a murderous assassin. We believe by being organized we can keep down violence or prevent it altogether. We are now dedicated to regaining our nation by purely political and educational means, as they are the means whereby a powerfully organized enemy nearly slipped the American Constitution away from us. The right aim of law is to prevent coercion either by force or by fraud. This is our battle-cry, and we are absolutely confident we shall restore respect for the Federal judiciary by replacing today's evil members

with Americans. We shall see men on the Supreme Court of the United States who feel to their nerve ends the high responsibility of their office to guard the Constitution, and to continue in the spirit of the Founding Fathers, and the American tradition of equal justice under the law.[23]
©1957 The University of Virginia

The preceding paragraph does not contain the paraphrased rants of a social demagogue. The rhetoric has neither been enhanced nor exaggerated through a critic's bias. The contents were not edited. Nothing was clipped from the paragraph nor was it altered in any way from the original. Those are John Kasper's exact words. They were included here to clearly indicate their viciousness, their cold-blooded inhumanity, and their riot-inducing objective. Imagine just saying out loud, never mind putting into print, that the justices of the United States Supreme Court, the "9 swine," should be dead, and it mattered not whether those deaths were by suicide, a mob lynching, or "a murderous assassin." These are the attitudes and beliefs which good, civil-minded people, people who wanted nothing but equality for all citizens, regardless of color, were having to deal with. Almost as if realizing the hostile nature of his words, Kasper tries to soften their potential for inciting violence by suggesting organized whites could achieve their objectives with "political and educational means." His efforts, however, were akin to a judge telling a jury to "disregard" some piece of testimony they've just heard—they really can't. It would be difficult if not impossible, to find more inflammatory and demagogic political commentary in print, than found in that one paragraph—even in today's huge social media marketplace, where anyone from a Rhodes scholar to an illiterate fool can write and post almost anything.

Was John Kasper mainstream? Was he speaking for and against a majority mindset? Probably not, but he was speaking to a large minority, one which was both loud and active. His words were inflammatory and

---

[23] Egerton

dangerous, aimed at a group of people who were feeling their power and influence slipping out of control, a group of people desperate to hang onto their way of life by any means possible...and desperate people will do desperate things.

Chapter Nine

John Kasper was not the sole voice of opposition, nor did all of the anti-integration rhetoric and sentiment racing across the South originate from without. In fact, the majority of the resistance movement came from within. In some segregationist organizations, for example the Tennessee Federation for Constitutional Government (TFCG), the slate of officers looked like a Who's Who list from Tennessee's uppermost echelons of high society, wealthy corporations, and ivy-league academia:

Chairman: Donald Davidson, English Professor,
Vanderbilt University
Vice-Chairman: Jack Kershaw, Nashville real estate developer
Vice-Chairman: L. V. DuBose, Production Control, A.V.C.O. Corp.,
Nashville
Secretary: Robert P. Lee, Assistant Business Manager,
Vanderbilt University
Treasurer: Gale, Smith and Company, Insurance of Nashville
Counsel: Paul F. Bumpus, former District Attorney-General
Dir. Public Relations: Paul T. Manchester, Professor and Dept. Head
for Romance Languages, Vanderbilt University

As previously stated, the TFCG was every bit as subversive as other white supremacist groups, but they appeared more reasonable and mainstream by "keeping the conversation at an adult level."[24] They took the same kind of racist, anti-integration positions as John Kasper, the Klan, and others—they were just nicer about it. While some groups and gatherings ranted and raved in the city square using street vernacular and vulgarity, the TFCG articulated their racism in position papers, using scholarly diction and syntax, or in intellectual speeches with school boards or other government agencies. These weren't men whose thoughts and beliefs were any better than folks who hid behind rocks, bottles, KKK robes, or anonymous letters, they just dressed better. Their message wasn't any different than the overt racists, it just sounded more educated.

---

[24] "We Kept the Discussion at an Adult Level."

For example, the street crowd of demonstrators might have screamed a mantra of "NOT ONE, NOT NOW, NOT EVER!" and waved their Confederate Flags to protest the integration of Clinton schools. However, in responding to the decision handed down by Judge Taylor in the lengthy suit by black students for admission to Clinton High School, a decision they saw as a victory for segregationists, the TFCG offered some rather polished commentary on the judge's ruling. In their October, 1955 newsletter the TFCG wrote how Judge Taylor essentially stated

> …*the NAACP cannot claim violation of "Good Faith" until "From and After" such time as arrangements have been made for admission on a non-discriminatory basis, which seemingly means until after a plan for desegregation has been adopted. Further and possibly indefinite postponement of admission of Negro pupils to Clinton High School seems likely."* [25]

"Not one, not now, not ever!" or "Further and possibly indefinite postponement of admission of Negro pupils to Clinton High School seems likely." The intellectual level of the discourse has obviously been raised in the TFCG excerpt, but the underlying message is about the same as that of the street thugs: we're better than you are; we deserve these schools—you don't; go back to Africa. When you strip it all down to the base level, white supremacists and their racist beliefs are what they are, whether they wear blue jeans and t-shirts or suit jackets and ties, no matter what kind of cars they drive, how much money is in their pockets, or how many degrees hang on their office walls.

---

[25] TFCG Special Newsletter to Members

Chapter Ten

It had been a long, hot summer in Nashville, the heart of middle Tennessee as well as its capital. Emotions were simmering along with the heat. Superintendent Bass and the Nashville Board of Education (BOE) were under a court ordered deadline to get Nashville schools desegregated. They were working diligently to make sure their elementary schools were all ready to take the first step of their plan.

The first "step" was the integration of all first-grade students on September 9, 1957. City schools would then take an additional step each year until the Plan was fully implemented, and all public schools K-12 were completely desegregated, which was to be by the start of the 1968-69 academic year. Even at its slow pace, however, the Plan would not move easily. Agitators who saw an opportunity to foment resistance and unrest— civil or uncivil—came to Nashville to do just that. White supremacists were determined to try and save the South and save whites in general from what they saw as the too-influential NAACP and the too-powerful United States Supreme Court.

Already having established himself a white supremacist radical, both in person and in print, John Kasper became a master at inciting anger and racism at any and all gatherings of like-minded folks. He moved across the South organizing rallies, parades, and demonstrations. Young, well-spoken, and white he could whip up a frenzy as fast as Mother Nature could whip up an Atlantic hurricane. From New Jersey he first went to Georgia. Then he took up residence in Washington, DC, before heading to Clinton, Tennessee, and eventually to Nashville. He simply could not resist trying to block the pending integration of Nashville Public Schools, the Athens of the South, and he inserted himself in myriad places all around the city. Any public elementary school which might open itself up to Negro students was fair game. Police, courts, judges, fines, cease and desist orders, nights in jail, seemingly nothing could deter Kasper from his objectives. Were the growing crowds joining the anti-integration movement or were they joining Kasper? There were probably some of both. It didn't matter to Kasper, though, so long as his name recognition was growing.

The vehemence of the resistance grew along with the numbers. Confederate Flags and signs like "KEEP OUR WHITE SCHOOLS

WHITE" were carried at Kasper's rallies. Parades included cars which carried signs and banners reading: "ACTION OF THE PRO-SOUTHERNERS," or "SOUTHERN WHITES ARE THE NEGROES' BEST FRIENDS… BUT NO INTEGRATION." Throughout the month of August 1957, the crowds got larger and the protesters more emboldened and virulent. The marches, demonstrations, and threats of violence increased as the opening day for school drew nearer. Membership in the Ku Klux Klan, the TFCG, and other white supremacist groups grew at an alarming rate.[26]

---

[26] Egerton

While most Nashville parents just wanted to abide by the law and have their children provided the best education possible, the opposition to integration was fierce. Segregationists drew strength from places like Little Rock, Arkansas, where integration met not just fierce but violent opposition. The Parents Preference Committee (PPC) was formed, which advocated for "The Parents Voluntary Plan." In an open letter to the parents of all Nashville students, the group pushed for a plan which they believed met the demands of the Supreme Court decision in Brown by closing the windows of forced segregation. But it would fling open the doors for voluntary segregation. The Parents Voluntary Plan allowed "there be no compulsory segregation in any grade; and there be no compulsory integration in any grade."[27] While the Plan did acknowledge "the 14th amendment of the Constitution protects equally the rights of all citizens, Negro and White," it went on to claim, "the 14th amendment does not force unwanted associations upon any citizen" (Letter to Nashville Parents).[28] The PPC would not give up easily. They knew their audience and they played to it.

In the era of anti-communism and anti-socialism, the Parents Voluntary Plan claimed it was grounded in democratic principles because, while it did not force integration neither did it force segregation, hence the not forcing "unwanted associations upon any citizen." "Every citizen," they chimed, "Negro and White, may exercise his free choice in a democratic manner."[29] And if that still wasn't enough, being in the heartland of the Bible-belt, the Committee included its proposition, "the plan conforms to the basic belief of the world's great religions: 'To love they (sic) neighbor as thyself' and 'To do unto others as you would have them do unto you' means 'respect thy neighbor's integrity and differences and be assured that he will respect yours, so that each may fully develop for the good of all."[30] One would be hard pressed to find a better perversion of the golden rule.

The segregationists even drew vicious public support from outside the South:

---

[27] Chester Mason
[28] Ibid.
[29] Ibid.
[30] Ibid.

AS A Sympathizer, let me suggest
That your school either place Negro
pupils in one room, whites in the
other... or if you seat them in ONE
room, seat whites on one side... colored
on the other...
Because... each has the right to
remember that God created them different,
black and white. And each would receive
equal education.

Try to reserve some states'rights.

The Nation as a whole is too-critical
Of Arkansas' Governor.

IF MR. WARREN HAD ANY GUTS HE
WOULD OUTLAW THE REAL TROUBLE*MAKER
IN THIS COUNTRY...THE NAACP.

A Citizen of California [31]

More probably the country was not hard enough on "Arkansas' (sic) Governor." Governor Faubus was a man who disobeyed both a court order and a presidential order. He turned the National Guard on his own citizens. He was a racist and white supremacist who believed not in the rule of law but in the law of rule—his rule. He did not walk softly, but he definitely carried a big stick, the biggest one he could find. Yet, there were those who thought "the nation as a whole [was] too critical of [him]." It was Faubus and others like him who buoyed the segregationists across the south, gave them cause for hope, a pattern of actions and behaviors to

---

[31] California Citizen. Anonymous.

were those who thought "the nation as a whole [was] too critical of [him]." It was Faubus and others like him who buoyed the segregationists across the south, gave them cause for hope, a pattern of actions and behaviors to copy, and examples to emulate. This is what black people, along with law-abiding white people were fighting against in Nashville.

Still, despite everything John Kasper and his supporters in the KKK, the TFCG, and the White Citizens' Council could do, despite the influences of local instigators and outside agitators and people so confident in the righteousness of their convictions they wouldn't even sign their name to them, despite all of that, the development of Nashville's plan continued. Like the proverbial tortoise, the pace was slow, but it was steady.

Chapter Eleven

Superintendent William Bass and Assistant Superintendent William Henry Oliver continued working diligently with the Nashville Board of Education throughout the summer of 1957, leading up to the opening of school in September. Ideas were floated. Proposals were offered. Motions were made, seconded, debated, and rejected. Amendments were tried, and along with them came passionate speeches for and against. Some motions passed, some didn't. The fundamental issue at stake was how to meet the mandates of the stair-step plan, bringing Nashville into compliance with *Brown,* without alienating parents and the general public. School officials did not want to risk a public backlash that could easily result in large scale riots and demonstrations. The last thing any of them wanted for Nashville was federal troops on its city streets or in its schoolyards.

Fortunately, Nashville schools were led by a team of administrators who believed the time had come for desegregation in public education, and who were committed to upholding the law. While he might have liked the process to bring about swift change, William Bass was all about "consensus—bringing people together, building mutual respect, and giving opponents room to work out their differences in a spirit of fairness and equity. Bass was looking ahead to his retirement at the end of 1957. His successor, already chosen, was to be Assistant Superintendent W. H. Oliver, who also served as principal of East High School. Through the fall and spring of the 1956-57 school year, the two men patiently guided the school board toward approval of a process by which desegregation would begin in the first grade in 1957 and extend to all twelve grades by 1968."[32] Their work was not easy and their contributions to Nashville's desegregation process should not be underestimated. Lesser men, men more concerned with their careers than with public service, might not have been able to pull it off. Straddling the line between one's conscience and public opinion is often a difficult and thankless task.

---

[32] Egerton

After a spring and summer of sweat, hard work, and some fear a policy took shape along with a plan for the opening of school. In August, the following letter was sent to the parents of all incoming first graders:

NASHVILLE CITY SCHOOLS
WILL HOLD ADVANCE REGISTRATION
FOR ALL FIRST GRADE STUDENTS ON
TUESDAY, AUGUST 27, 1957

All first-grade students who expect to attend the Nashville City Schools this fall will please report with their parents or guardians on Tuesday, August 27, 1957, at 8:30 a.m., to the schools they expect to attend this fall.

Let the parent make sure the student has with him his or her birth certificate and certificate of immunizations. The City law requires immunization against smallpox. In addition, they should present evidence of the fact they have been inoculated against typhoid fever and polio and have been given the multiple antigen vaccine against whooping cough, tetanus, and diphtheria as required by the Davidson County Board of Health.

Each first grade student will be expected to attend school in his own zone unless the majority of the students in his grade or in that school are of another race, and the parent requests transfer for this reason. Every first-grade student has the privilege of attending school in his own zone, regardless of race, if his parents so desire, but no student will be required to attend a school in which the majority of the students are of another race.

Prior to the advance registration to be held on August 27, parents who desire to have their children transferred to a school outside their zone, in order that they may attend school with members of their own race, may request such transfer by letter or by telephone (Chapel 2-5575). The child should take this letter with him when he reports for registration on August 27.

The purpose of the advance registration is to enable principals and teachers to administer more adequately to the needs of each individual child, as well as for the parents. It is desirable to make this day as pleasant and as profitable as possible. To this end, the cooperation of everyone concerned is earnestly requested.

Wm. Henry Oliver
Assistant Superintendent
Approved: W.A. Bass Superintendent[33]

The two men did everything in their power to keep things moving forward in a reasonable, prudent, and competent manner. They tried to maintain a calmness and sense of normalcy even as the tensions throughout the city rose. They executed their duties with professionalism, letting all associated with the Nashville School District know schools would open on September 9, 1957, they would do so with all possible sensitivity to the needs of their students and parents, but they would do so in compliance with law.

---

[33] Bass, Oliver. "Letter for Advance Registration."

Chapter Twelve

While the Boards of Education and the politicians were wrestling with the legalities of integration vs segregation, of Constitutional law vs states' rights, of plans, resolutions, and appeals, local school personnel—faculty, staff, and administrators—were going about the business of education. Teachers worked on gathering books and preparing materials for their classrooms, writing lesson plans, decorating bulletin boards, and arranging desks. Office staff prepared lists and files for new students and updated those for returning students. Administrators tried to fill vacant positions. Janitors and lunch-room workers cleaned, waxed, polished, and stocked as they got rooms and facilities ready for fall. The average member of the public, even most parents and students, have little idea how much goes on to get ready for the first day of school each fall.

As instructed by Superintendent Bass, every elementary school in Nashville was also preparing for the advance registration day. Most everyone was a bit more anxious than usual, given the public uproar over desegregation, but they all still had jobs to do, and a major one was preparing for the first day of school. Ready or not several thousand students were going to show up for the start of classes on September 9th, and approximately ten percent of them would be brand new first graders, most of whom had never been to any kind of school before.

Come August 27th, the day all first graders in the city were asked to pre-register at the schools they would be attending in the fall, tensions were running high, and nerves were stretched far beyond the normal pre-opening jitters. The days always flew by fast in August, leaving too many things to do with too few days left in which to do them, but this year was different. No one knew exactly what to expect, yet they sensed whatever "it" was, it wouldn't be good.

Over on the East side of the city, Glenn School had been watched the most carefully by the segregationists. Approximately twenty-five black six-year-olds lived within its school zone, and therefore demonstrators were out in force. Many of those who dared to pre-register were harassed, threatened, and bullied. Tires were burned in the streets. Bottles, cans, even rocks were thrown from their hands, while the vilest of epithets were thrown from their mouths. Still, a few brave and determined parents did make the decision to register their children early, despite the dangerous and fearful conditions. Sadly, though, even some of those who braved the preregistration never actually arrived on opening day, so severe was the intimidation: warnings of kidnappings, promises to burn homes, even death threats.

In a nearby school zone, the family of six-year-old Era Mae Bailey, who had preregistered her at the previously all-white Bailey School, decided the risk of attending Bailey was too great. After receiving a letter from the Ku Klux Klan threatening cross burnings if they didn't move, the child's grandparents, her legal guardians, sent her to an all-black school instead.[34]

In the days following registration, "anonymous" adults had been around to every elementary school in the city and spoken with an administrator to find out if any "Negro children" had registered. Two six-year-old black children had preregistered at Glenn Elementary; at Jones Elementary there were four. At Buena Vista three black children signed up, and at Fehr four had come in. By the time early registration was over a total of fifteen black students were enrolled in seven schools which had been all-white. On opening day four more would join them. Nineteen black first-graders, would take their first fearful steps into school—and into history.

Those nineteen little kids and their parents would ultimately receive quite an education that first day—and much of it would happen outside of any formal classroom. Ultimately, whether the first step of Nashville's stair-step plan for desegregation would succeed or fail depended "not on white acceptance but on black courage."[35] Those black parents, those children, they didn't give speeches in opposition to their party. They didn't take figurative steps of unpopular political positions or votes. They took literal steps. They knowingly put themselves in harm's way. They suffered the wrath of their white brethren. They heard the racist slurs, felt the rocks and bottles, and wiped off the spittle. Those families risked their lives to help right a grievous wrong, and in doing so help build a better America.

---

[34] Egerton
[35] Ibid.

Talk about courage. They are the ones who should have been profiled for a book on acts of courage, not a bunch of United States Senators, who in actuality risked little more than their careers.[36]

---

[36] John F. Kennedy, Profiles in Courage

PART TWO
(The Nashville School District)

The enemy is fear. We think it is hate;
but, it is fear.

—Mahatma Gandhi

Chapter Thirteen

One of the people involved in all kinds of preparation for school that summer was MaryAnne Bruce. MaryAnne's level of enthusiasm for the upcoming year at Hattie Cotton was off the scale. Everything was new and exciting: new school, new community, new colleagues, new principal, new students, and most importantly, a new beginning. She was thrilled at the possibilities for this fresh start.

Teaching had actually been MaryAnne's second career choice. By her junior year in high school, she was determined she was going to nursing school, obtain her RN, and become a nurse-missionary in Africa. Some missionaries assigned to the Congo had come to speak at the church where her father was pastor and the young MaryAnne Williams had been greatly inspired. Ever the practical guide, MaryAnne's mother insisted she get a job in a doctor's office the summer between her junior and senior years. The doctor she worked for was extremely impressed with MaryAnne's level of dedication, work ethic, and empathy for the patients. She was a "natural" for nursing school. Things couldn't have gotten much better—until one of her high school friends was brought into the clinic following a bad car accident. Pregnant and bleeding profusely from multiple areas of her body, MaryAnne took one good look at the girl and fainted—literally passed out. A career in nursing, at home or abroad, was not going to happen.

Still wanting to be a missionary, MaryAnne decided she would become a missionary teacher rather than a missionary nurse. Therefore, instead of enrolling in Cookeville Hospital's nursing program, she headed off to Martin College to become a math teacher. While there, toward the end of her freshman year, each student in MaryAnne's dorm "adopted" an underprivileged child from the neighboring town of Pulaski to act as a sort of big sister/mentor. MaryAnne quickly discovered how much she loved working with children, and how much she enjoyed reading to them and helping them learn to read and write. It seemed a natural for missionary work.

Around the same time MaryAnne also found herself enjoying the company of a seminary student named Ralph Bruce. And while he had a great deal of interest in MaryAnne, sadly he had no interest in being a foreign missionary. And so, once they married her career trajectory shifted again—this time from mission work in Africa to elementary education in America. In the end, it was the right change, for it led her to all of the "new" she was preparing for at Hattie Cotton.

However, Hattie Cotton was year number two. One of the things MaryAnne was so looking forward to in her second year of teaching was a "new beginning." Prior to the upcoming year at Hattie Cotton there had been year number one, and that year had not been nearly so exciting. Rather it had been...well, let's hear about it from her.

Chapter Fourteen

I started teaching in Nashville in the fall of 1956, fresh out of college and ready to take on the world of public education. Martin College, University of Chattanooga, Tennessee Tech, and my recent wedding were all behind me. Before school opened the fall after I graduated Tennessee Tech I had a job! My very first contract, all $3,050.00 of it, was to teach third grade at McCann Elementary, and…let's just say round one went to McCann. I was miserable that year. I felt a little bit like Job from the Bible must have felt—presented with test after difficult test and losing every one of them. My first year of teaching was so bad it's little short of a miracle I ever had a second one.

First of all, the school was in a fairly tough area of town, over near the state prison. It was an impoverished neighborhood with an unusually transient population. It seemed like my students were constantly moving. They would move into a house or apartment, fall behind on rent, get evicted, and then start over again a few blocks away…again, and again. Most families could barely make ends meet, and many couldn't.

Discipline was a daily challenge. Remember, I was a brand-new teacher, so I didn't have a bag of tricks, no experience to fall back on. Wanting to get off to a good start with my students, I tried not to be the stereotypical children-in-straight-rows-hands-folded-on-top-of-desks-mouths-closed-school-marm-type of old-school teacher—big mistake. I had kids up out of their chairs, moving around the room constantly. They talked and laughed and played around almost as much as they worked. I had one girl, I think her name might have been Anna Mae,* who was just determined she would do whatever she wanted whenever she wanted. She was so loud, and delighted in making my life miserable. The more I tried to rein her in the more she pushed back. It was a constant, daily battle. And the farther into the year we went, the worse things got.

Think about this: I had done my student teaching in a "Demonstration School." The students were hand-picked, motivated learners, and highly disciplined. They could have…well, they could have almost taught themselves. Few if any of the veteran teachers at McCann had much interest in helping me. For one thing, they had enough of their own challenges. And don't forget, I was the new kid, the college graduate, fresh from the latest textbooks—why would I need any help? But the most troubling issue I faced was one which could literally have doomed my career almost before it got started, I did not have the support of my building principal.

Never will I forget the day I got a message to go see the principal, right in the middle of a class. I was already nervous, I mean it was most irregular to get called out of a class, so by the time I got to her office I was really on edge. The secretary told me to go right in. I opened the door and there stood a serious looking Principal Jones* and Anna Mae's mother, who looked positively enraged. I had to stand there and listen to this woman accuse me of hating her daughter and not knowing how to deal with her. She claimed I hated her so much I had locked her in a closet with no handle on the inside because I didn't know what else to do with her. She said her daughter was so upset by it all, and hated me so much, she didn't even want to come back to school, and she certainly didn't want to ever be in my classroom again. Her final insult was that I was so bad I shouldn't even be a teacher; I should just be fired.

What really distressed me the most about the entire, humiliating ordeal wasn't even the completely fabricated story Anna Mae had told her mother, or that her mother clearly believed it. What really did me in was Mrs. Jones's response: "If you want her fired, put what you just told me in writing, I will bring it to the superintendent, and she will be fired." I was so shocked at what I was hearing I don't think I said much in response, other than to respectfully deny locking anyone in a closet and offer my apologies to her and her daughter for being so upset.

I really could not believe what had just happened, and if I hadn't been witness to it, I probably wouldn't have believed it. The only thing I wanted was to be a good teacher. Now, after four years of college, a semester of student teaching, and a few months into my very first job, it all appeared to be in serious jeopardy. I knew I was not on Anna Mae's "list of favorite teachers," but to make up such a lie was…truthfully, I had never experienced anything like it. And her mother—to believe I would actually do such a thing. Unbelievable.

After I got home from school, following some dismay, some anger, some tears, and some cooling off I called the superintendent's office. I explained my situation, trying not to sound accusatory but needing to convey the fact that McCann Elementary and I were just not a good fit, that I was not having a successful first-year experience, and if at all possible I wanted a transfer. I am guessing Anna Mae's mother never put anything in writing, because I was not fired, and, thankfully, Mrs. Jones supported my transfer request. By the time everything got *settled it was late spring, so we all agreed I would finish the 1956/57 school year at McCann. For the next year, however, I was assigned to the Hattie Cotton Elementary School in East Nashville. I didn't know anything about it, but I knew it was in a good section of the city, I knew it was a much shorter commute for me from Gallatin, and I knew it wasn't McCann.*

* Not a real name

Chapter Fifteen

There had been a lot of unrest during the summer of 1957, and not just in Nashville. The cities of Knoxville and Clinton had their troubles as well: Knoxville mostly in the courts and Clinton mostly in the streets. Beyond Tennessee there were protests and demonstrations in Alabama, Arkansas, Mississippi, Georgia, most everywhere across the South. Fear, deepening anger, and frustration were spreading across the land faster than Kudzu was spreading beside the highways. Waving signs and banners like "Keep Our White Schools White," Klansmen, along with other white groups and white parents, were fighting desperately to prevent the desegregation of public schools.

During the last week before school was scheduled to open, it seemed like every edition of the daily papers and every nightly news broadcast brought reports of more demonstrations, more disturbances, and more calls for whites to resist integration of their schools. Images of burning tires in the streets played across television screens. Negroes were scorned and harassed much more openly. One photograph featured a black man kissing a white woman under a headline which in part read, "Last Days of Peace Between white and Nigra Races; white Citizens Said To Be Arming!" Several white citizen's groups, along with the KKK, were drawing increasingly large and unruly crowds. By late August things were getting scary. Near riot conditions existed in many Nashville school yards and streets, even on the Capitol Building steps, as the time for school opening came closer. There was speculation Governor Clement might have to call out the Tennessee National Guard to help maintain the rule of law.[37]

The worst of the agitators, John Kasper, was prepped and on his game. Even though the rallies and marches he had organized around many of the schools to disrupt preregistration had failed in that objective, he was by no means giving up. He continued to speak all around the city, using

---

[37] "Blast Wrecks School."

his formidable skills of oratory to instill self-righteous anger in whites and mortal fear in blacks. And while he may have been the most visible, Kasper wasn't alone in his beliefs or his racist rhetoric.

The Rev. Fred Stroud, a defrocked Presbyterian minister and ally of Kasper, was also a vehement segregationist. One Nashville congregation had the good sense to send him packing, so he turned around and started his own congregation, the Bible Presbyterian Church. Yes, unbelievably, the Bible Presbyterian Church. Stroud used God and the Bible to defend segregation in the 1950s just like slave owners had used God and the Bible to defend slavery in the 1850s, and for centuries before that. This man didn't just offer his own views, he preached God's views. He really believed the signs he endorsed: "Segregation is the will of God"; "God is the author of Segregation." In one period photograph, Stroud is holding a sign which reads: "Communists Infiltrated our Churches, Now it (sic) Integrates our schools --2nd Peter 2: 1-2."[38] One must assume the "communists" (the biblical false prophets referred to in 2nd Peter) who had "[i]nfiltrated [their] churches and were integrat[ing their] schools" were the Godless Supreme Court justices, whose works were being carried out by the equally Godless police and politicians. Surely it was obvious to every white citizen, who would need to use only a small amount of their God-given brain, the presence of lack students into "[their] white schools" was going to be the end of public education and the ruination of America, perhaps of civilization itself. (Please forgive me reader, but I find blunt sarcasm does occasionally serve to better drive home a point than does scholarly diction and syntax.)

Such was the social atmosphere during the summer of 1957. Forces were at work trying to bring about havoc and chaos to the buildings and classrooms where MaryAnne Bruce and hundreds of her colleagues would soon be working with the hearts and minds of Nashville's young. While teachers were preparing to help students develop literacy and wisdom, others were preparing to sow bigotry and hatred. Public schools in Nashville were under assault, and it wasn't a few black first-graders who were the assailants. It wasn't the NAACP or Earl Warren or the entire U.S. Supreme Court. Bigoted, racist, white supremacists were the ones leading the attack, and so far they had been relentless.

---

[38] "Blast Wrecks School."

Chapter Sixteen

During that late summer, as I watched the news from Nashville, I couldn't help but think back to some of the racism I had observed first-hand in my life. I married my first husband, Ralph Bruce, a Methodist minister, in 1955, the year before I graduated college. Right after our wedding we moved to Crossville, Tennessee in Cumberland County, which prided itself on being a white county. In fact, it had an unofficial slogan: "The sun doesn't set on a nigger in Cumberland County." Surely it was just some made-up story—at least I hoped so. But my father-in-law was in retail, and I shall never forget the night he was talking about one of the salesmen he dealt with at Hills, the department store he managed. He was recalling a day when one of his salesmen was almost too late to get his merchandise delivered and get down the mountain in time. "Get down the mountain in time for what?" I asked. He replied, "In time so he and his nigra driver were out of Cumberland County before the sun went down." I almost couldn't believe what I was hearing.

I also remember sitting with some of Ralph's parishioners one Sunday afternoon at their dining room table. They had asked us to their home for dinner after church. Sensing Ralph was not particularly fond of the desert they had served, they asked him if he had a favorite desert. He said, "Well, to tell you the truth, the thing I like best is Nigger Toes and saltines." Even then the term bothered me, and I told him so. We agreed from that point on we would call them chocolate drops. Of course, most people had no idea what we were talking about when we said chocolate drops, and when we tried to explain they simply responded, "Oh, you mean Nigger Toes."

I thought about another time when I was younger. My mother had undergone surgery for breast cancer. Though we had all been scared, considering the time period, the surgery itself had gone well. The recuperation time, however, was going to be substantial. We needed someone to help us for several weeks, not just with care for my mother but to get meals and take care of the house. I think someone in my father's church recommended Betty, and she was a dream. She cooked, she cleaned, and she kept my mother from doing all the things she shouldn't! What's sad is, I never knew her full name, because everyone just called her Brown Betty. She would not use the front door of our house, but always entered and left by the back. She would not eat at the table with us, even when I begged her to do so, nor would she eat until after we had finished. I asked her *once if I could wait and eat with her. She said, "No, Miss MaryAnne, that's not my place." I was really too young to understand what she meant, but she said it with conviction, so I didn't argue.*

During most of my high school years we lived in Carthage, Tennessee. There was a mixed-race couple living on a farm just outside of town. I don't remember much about them—don't think I ever even knew very much—except he was white and she was black, and a whole lot of people treated them very badly. They hardly ever dared to come into town together. And when one or the other did have to come in they were taunted and harassed so much they feared for their lives. Finally, one night the KKK came and set fire to a cross in their front yard. The man and woman were so frightened they left their home and never returned.

Chapter Seventeen

Those weren't the only times MaryAnne encountered blatant racism, either. She and Ralph left Tennessee sometime in July of 1958 for New England, so Ralph could attend Boston University. They actually ended up living in a small town in New Hampshire called Penacook, just outside of the capitol city, Concord. For the next three years Ralph served the Penacook Methodist Church.

Shortly after MaryAnne and Ralph made their move to New Hampshire, MaryAnne's parents also moved. Her father had been appointed to pastor a church in Nashville, Tulip Street Methodist Church. So, when MaryAnne and Ralph returned to Tennessee for vacation the next summer they were eager to see her folks' new house and church. Even though they stayed first with Ralph's parents, Tulip Street Church wasn't far away, so they decided to make the drive out there on their first Sunday back in Tennessee and surprise her parents, who weren't expecting them at their house for another week-and-a-half.

They arrived a little early for worship and decided to wait on the sidewalk in front of the church until her folks got there. That way they could go in together and sit with her mother. What they didn't know was there was quite a conversation going on inside amongst the ushers. You see, unlike most southern clergy in those days, Ralph had decided he would wear a clerical collar. About the only time southerners saw one of those, the clergyperson was one of two things, a Roman Catholic priest or a northern rabble rouser come down to take up the cause of civil rights for blacks. All the ushers saw were two people they didn't recognize standing on the sidewalk out front, obviously waiting for someone, or something. They had never met MaryAnne or Ralph, it was a protestant church, and so the ushers assumed they were coming to help force the issue of accepting blacks into their congregation.

If it wasn't so sad it would have been almost comical when the head usher came out and introduced himself. Before he found out anything about them, he started telling them they didn't want any kind of trouble, and if they were waiting for some Negroes they had a list of parishioners who were willing to sit beside them. Let me say he was more than a little embarrassed when MaryAnne and Ralph listened to him with a what-are-you-talking-about look on their faces. Then they introduced themselves as the minister's daughter and her husband who were visiting from New Hampshire. They continued, saying they were simply waiting for her parents to arrive before they went in. The poor man could not apologize, welcome them, and excuse himself fast enough. But I am getting ahead of the story.

Chapter Eighteen

In an effort to avoid mosquitos, chiggers, and sunburns, but mostly unruly crowds, I spent as much time as I could at home that summer in front of fans and open windows learning about Hattie Cotton Elementary School. I talked on the phone and in person with friends, family members, and colleagues. I learned the school, located on Greenwood Avenue in East Nashville, was only a few years old, having opened its doors in 1950. It had been named for a beloved former Nashville teacher and academic supervisor in the early part of the twentieth-century, Miss Hattie R. Cotton.

It seemed Miss Cotton, or Miss Hattie as the kids called her, had taught both the chairman of the city board of education and one of the architects who designed the new school, Joseph Holman, of Marr and Holman. According to a Nashville Banner article Miss Hattie R. Cotton, was a beloved teacher, "popular with the board of education, the parents, and the children." She was a native Nashvillian who began her teaching career somewhere around 1900 and retired in 1924 after teaching an estimated 4,000 students. Someone actually recalled, as a "fond" memory "she wasn't averse to backing up her orders with a sharp rap across the palm with a ruler."

The building itself, according to all, was beautiful. In addition to the well-furnished modern classrooms, the school had a huge lunchroom, a well-equipped library, and outside there was a big playground. Classrooms had enough seats for all the students, a teacher's desk, chalkboards and bulletin boards. Each one also had its own bathroom, which I could hardly believe, along with built-in storage and supply cabinets.

One of the best things I learned during all of my summer research on Hattie Cotton, though I didn't realize then just how good it would be, was that Irene Spivy would be my buddy teacher. Since there were two classes for each grade level, the two teachers were referred to as "buddy teachers." The person I was replacing had retired at the end of the previous school year, so Irene and I would have the sixth grade. Everything I found out served to excite me all the more. I just knew this year was going to be a lot different than last, and I couldn't wait to get started.

---

[39] "New School To Honor Memory of Beloved Teacher." The Nashville Room. Nashville Public Library

Chapter Nineteen

Following pre-registration day, angst, anguish, and unabated fury were on display all over Nashville, because of the fifteen black children who had registered in previously all-white schools. The segregationists saw it not as losing fifteen seats, but as losing a way of life. And for many, avoiding such an outcome was worth any price—demonstrations, sit-ins, violence—whatever it took. Fortunately, there were some rational people in positions of leadership around the city.

Superintendent of Schools Bass and Assistant Superintendent Oliver knew there could be no more delays in bringing their schools into compliance with the Supreme Court mandate on integration. Once its passage was assured, the two administrators kept gentle forward pressure on the stair-step plan, moving it ever closer to the September 9th opening day of classes. Many people in their final year before retirement look to sort of coast through those last twelve months and pass off any remaining trouble spots to their successor. Superintendent Bass, however, did not waver in his professional duties, clearly seeing them as his civic and moral duties as well.

Mayor Ben West, criticized by many for his pro-integration stance, had publicly stated following the Brown ruling that "all of our citizens are entitled to the opportunity of an education, and I am sure our board of education will protect all in this right." West also refused to acquiesce to the Parent's School Preference Committee's demands to disavow integration, and further declared, again in public, his own six-year-old son would be starting first grade at Ransom Elementary, one of the potential schools to be desegregated. [40]

Governor Clement was also one of those rational leaders. Of the many bills introduced and passed by the state legislature to delay integration, most of the ones not ruled unconstitutional by the courts were vetoed by Clement. He was criticized by many as a "nigger lover." But

---

[40] Egerton

no matter what else he might have believed in or used for guidance, the governor believed in upholding the law, and in Tennesseans as law abiding citizens—and desegregation of public schools was the law.

MaryAnne was about to personally encounter another one of those rational leaders at the Hattie Cotton School, where in a couple of weeks she would begin her second year as a teacher. That person was Principal Margaret Cate. Having devoted much of her life to education, public and private, Miss Cate was a person of high moral character and unquestionable integrity. MaryAnne would learn, in a powerful, first-hand way, just how devoted Miss Cate was to the people she served, both her students and her faculty. She would also experience just how devoted they were to Miss Cate. There is no doubt Miss Hattie R. Cotton would be pleased to see her namesake led by Margaret R. Cate. In fact, it will not be at all surprising to someday see a group of Nashville students attending the Margaret R. Cate Elementary School.

Chapter Twenty

I was a little nervous the first day I drove over to Hattie Cotton to meet Margaret Cate. I was fairly sure she would have heard about my struggles the year before. In addition, I knew she hadn't really had a choice about my coming to Hattie Cotton, because the Superintendent had just assigned me there. I didn't want her to think I would be a problem for her—and Lord knows I didn't want another bad year. On the other hand, she had mentioned me in her pre-school letter to teachers in a way which sounded very positive and welcoming. Still, even though going to meet her was my idea, my nerves were just a bit on edge.

I left Gallatin in my black and white Ford Fairlane which we had bought the year before. It was the first car I had ever had with air conditioning, so even though it was a hot Tennessee summer morning, at least my body was comfortable. My mind was a different story. For most of the half-hour drive it was occupied with "what will she be like…what will the school be like…will she be as kind and 'motherly' as I had heard …will she like me …I wonder what she has heard about me …" So busy were my thoughts in almost no time I was in East Nashville and turning off Greenwood Avenue into the graveled parking lot. As I got out of the car and gazed around, I was struck by the neatness of the school building and the neighborhood into which it was nestled even more than the heat.

Looking to my left across Greenwood Ave., the street was lined with small but well-kept single-family houses. Most were wood and block construction. Almost all had gravel driveways and covered front porches with swings or rocking chairs or both. Some of them had a fence along the street with a gate at the front walk. The grass was trimmed, and the yards were mostly free of clutter. And there must have been a Mimosa still in bloom somewhere nearby because I swear I can remember my nose starting to itch as I stood there looking around.

To my right was the school I had heard so much about. I knew the building to be about seven years old, but to me, the modern brick and glass exterior appeared almost brand new. I smoothed the front of my light blue pima cotton dress, flipped a small stone out of my white sandals and made my way across the gravels to the cement pad. I opened the front door, stepped inside my new school, and headed in the direction of the main office to meet the woman I had heard so much about.

To the casual observer, Margaret Cate might have seemed …unremarkable. Yet, upon introduction she impressed me. She radiated professionalism, decorum, and class. She was wearing an understated, light pink dress with a lace collar, and had short gray hair neatly brushed toward the back. There was no secretary in the office that day, so she opened her door herself, greeted me, and invited me to come in and sit down. She calmed my jitters almost immediately by mentioning we had something in common. Pleasantly surprised I asked, "What is that?" "I see your husband is the pastor of Lambuth Methodist church," she replied. "I live on the other side of town and attend West End Methodist. I taught Sunday school there for years, and even wrote a couple of children's books to teach in Sunday School." We chatted casually for several minutes about people we both knew from church. I had known Rauzelle Johnson, one of her associate pastors for years, and Farris Moore, her church's District Superintendent, was a long-time family friend, going back to my father's days in seminary. The pleasant conversation further eased my concerns and calmed my jitters. Then, almost as if to get it out of the way, she remarked, "I understand you had a difficult time last year. Do you want to talk about it?" And I did.

I tried very hard to be honest without being harshly so. I needed and wanted to tell her the truth, all of it, but to also let her know I had every confidence I could be a good teacher, and not come across like I was blaming everyone else for my troubles. I talked about the transient nature of the school's student population, the stark differences between the realities at McCann and the training I had received. I talked some about the neighborhood surrounding the school and its proximity to the State Prison, where one or the other parent of many McCann students was incarcerated. I talked about some of the things I had learned, even though they might have been negatives. They were still learning experiences, from which I could extract information to help make me a better teacher. And, yes, I did tell her in as gentle terms as I could about the incident involving my principal, the upset parent, and me. That's when Miss Cate really impressed me. She never uttered a derogatory word about her colleague, never rolled her eyes, or even raised an eyebrow. She did, however, as she rose up out of her chair, get this ever-so-slight hint of a smile, along with the vaguest glint in her eyes which told me, "That sounds about right." What she actually said was. "Well, MaryAnne, let's go show you the school," and off we went.

The building, I could see, was laid out sort of like a giant "E." As you faced it from outside, across the long front were the lunchroom to the left, the main entrance doors and office area in the middle, and the library to the right. Then, each of the three "legs," heading toward the rear playground, housed the classrooms: the left was for grades one and two, the middle for three and four, and my wing, grades five and six, was on the right behind the library. There were four classrooms in each wing. Every classroom had a row of windows on one side and the door to the hallway on the opposite. And at the end of each hallway was a door to the playground.

Before I left, Miss Cate gave me a complete set of the Teacher Edition textbooks I would need, so I could become familiar with them. By the time we made it back to the front doors I was completely at ease and eager to get started. Instead of being worried about what had happened last year, I was getting excited about what could happen this year. My ride home was a whole lot more relaxed than my ride in.

Chapter Twenty-One

That early meeting with Margaret Cate was incredibly valuable to MaryAnne—a real boost to her self-confidence. Not only did it help her begin to feel a part of the school community, but it also provided a needed distraction from what had happened to her professionally the year before. A bad first year as a teacher can be as crippling to an entire career as a bad first year of school can be damaging to a child's entire education. It also helped take her mind off some of what was going on throughout greater Nashville, which just seemed to keep getting worse. The agitators continued looking for trouble. Where there wasn't any, they had learned how to create it. Their menu of hate and discontent was extensive, and the appetites of their patron followers seemingly insatiable.

The trip to Hattie Cotton, however, had helped MaryAnne refocus on beginning her second year of teaching in the Nashville School System. The social unrest notwithstanding, this school year had all the promise of great success. The modern, well-equipped school was such a huge difference from the aging McCann, but her meeting had revealed something much more important—and reassuring: Miss Cate. Margaret had been nothing but genuinely kind, gracious, and professional throughout their get-acquainted session. She had revealed herself to be a caring and compassionate principal, one MaryAnne knew she could count on for any help or guidance she might need. In one brief meeting she had helped MaryAnne put the previous year where it belonged—in the past. Perhaps the most important thing Margaret had done for her newest faculty member was reaffirm MaryAnne's belief in her career choice.

Margaret also confirmed everything MaryAnne had heard about her buddy teacher, Miss Spivy, assuring her she would find Irene most supportive and eager to be helpful in any way. Additionally, she talked about the rest of the faculty, and did so in such a way as to clearly indicate she was proud of her staff and respected each and every member of it. She worked into the conversation various ways in which they collaborated, particularly the buddy teachers within each grade. She talked not only about their shared professional respect for each other but their personal regard for one another as well. All things worked together so as not only to settle down MaryAnne's concerns but dramatically ratchet up her excitement for the start of school, and being a part of Hattie Cotton.

Chapter Twenty-Two

*C*lasses were not beginning for another week, but I couldn't wait any longer. I just had to get started setting up my room and planning for the new year in my new school. The integration protests were getting worse around the city, drawing larger and increasingly violent crowds, but I was so happy and excited I could hardly contain myself. Actually, I'm not sure I did contain myself very well. I imagine most of my family and a lot of my friends were pretty darn tired of hearing me babble about the start of school. So, I made my second trip in less than a week from Gallatin to Nashville, but this time with no worry, only excitement and anticipation.

When I arrived at school, I let Miss Cate know I was there and would be working in my room—my room! I remember sitting at my desk for the longest time, just looking around the space and thinking about what I would put where: how I might arrange the desks, decorate the bulletin boards and walls. The only thing up in the room at that point was the twenty-six card Zaner Bloser cursive alphabet chart, which took up the top of two walls, the one thing linking most every elementary classroom in America. I had a lot of work to do to make this classroom a home—but I also had a lot of ideas.

I didn't really want to place my desk in front of the students' desks, all in precise rows, but I also didn't want to appear to be a renegade, the young newbie with all the "new and improved" ideas, and better ways of doing things. So, I set my room up in a fairly conventional manner. I found other ways to inject some color and personality into the rather bland classroom. I covered my bulletin boards with yellow construction paper. I made a September calendar large enough that we could write quite a bit on any given day. I made a sign for the wall which read "STUDENT WORK," where I could later hang their papers, and another which said, "HELPER OF THE DAY." Then I made smaller ones, each with a student's name on them that would be hung underneath. And I made everything with the loudest colors of construction paper I could find—anything to brighten up the plain beige walls and gray floor tiles.

I had most of my set-up and decorating done by the time I left on Tuesday. By Wednesday, most of the other teachers began arriving, including my buddy teacher. Irene was a gem, and I liked her right away. She was a small lady; I mean fairly short and slender. She had short graying curls and *dressed very conservatively, often a button-down, collared blouse with a straight dark skirt and matching pumps. Almost before our introduction was complete she began to make me feel at home, and I don't mean by saying "hello" and bringing me a cup of coffee. I mean in much more practical ways. She showed me where to get supplies like pencils, paper, chalk, and erasers. She took me to the teacher's room where the Ditto machine was and showed me how to use it, and how to fill it with the nasty smelling fluid.[41] She showed me how she set up her register and attendance lists. She took me through the lunchroom and the library and out to the playground at the back of the building. She also went over how she taught a number of the lessons we would be teaching in the first few weeks: how she grouped students for reading; how she blocked regions of the United States, and countries of the world for geography; what had worked best for her in teaching how to multiply and divide fractions.*

What really amazed me about Irene, though, was she didn't stop her sharing with just professional matters. When we weren't working on curriculum, lesson plans, or other school matters, she shared of herself personally, too, and I discovered a number of things we had in common. Irene was what we called in those days an "old maid." She actually lived in Estill Springs, Tennessee, and just kept a small apartment in Nashville where she stayed during the week. On Fridays she went back to Estill Springs where she cared for her aging parents. Estill Springs is near Carthage, where I graduated high school. We talked about people and places we both knew, like my high school friend Ruth Jean McCall, whose parents owned McCall's Appliance Store, and Tuley Furniture Company owned by my friend Bob Tuley's parents. I told her the Tuley's were members of the Carthage Methodist Church where my father was the pastor at the time. I also recalled the Gores were members of my father's church and I had been invited to the Gore farm outside of Carthage several times for a Sunday meal or birthday party. Al Gore Sr. was a senator then, so he often wasn't around. His son, Al Jr. was just a little boy, but I was pretty good friends with his daughter Nancy.

We talked about going to the tent revivals that often came to town, and sometimes driving out to the Negro tent revivals to sit in the car and listen to the singing, which was wonderful. My family moved from Carthage the year I

---

[41]Spirit duplicator or mimeograph

started college, so she caught me up on who had died since I'd lived there, how the area had grown, what things had changed, and what things were pretty much the same. Hacket's Drug Store was still there on Main Street in the courthouse square, as was every town's favorite, Woolworth's Department Store. Irene was more than a colleague, more than a friend; she really was a "buddy."

Chapter Twenty-Three

Almost before she knew it, MaryAnne's week of preparation was done. By the time she was ready to head back to Gallatin Friday afternoon, the staff meetings and planning sessions were over, and the jitters were gone, having been replaced by excitement and anticipation for the arrival of students. Her roster and registers were all set up, and her rows of desks had been adjusted, at least twice. In one corner of her desk sat the folder with her first week of lesson plans. On the chalkboard she had written in the upper left-hand corner, using three lines of near perfect cursive: *Mrs. Bruce, Grade 6, September 9, 1957.* She had neatly placed textbooks on each student's desk: their reading book, science book, geography text, and their math book. She also included a notebook for writing practice. She had even put up the name of her first helper of the day. Before closing the door to leave, she quickly recapped the week's activities in her mind, took a look around the room, did a quick mental check list for day one, and suddenly realized…she was ready.

What she didn't fully realize was the forces at work trying to disrupt the first day were also ready—ready for the final two-day push to derail integration, no matter what it took. John Kasper chose the grounds of the War Memorial Building for the setting of his rally on Sunday, September 8th, the night before schools opened. Seriously—the War Memorial Building. The man who had already predicted "blood will run in the streets of Nashville if nigra children go to school with whites!" just continued to turn up the heat, along with the rhetoric. Speaking to a crowd of some three hundred supporters and sympathizers "Our country was born in violence," Kasper exhorted. "Tomorrow is the day. Every blow you strike will be a blow for freedom." Freedom for some, perhaps, but he obviously didn't mean freedom for everyone. But it still wasn't enough, for he added, "I say that integration can be reversed. It has got to be a pressure down here which is more or less like a lit stick of dynamite, and you throw it in their laps and let them catch it, and then they can do what they want with it—let them worry about that." [42]

---

[42]Egerton

It is difficult to imagine how sowing the seeds of hate from so few could take root in the hearts and minds of so many. Those few rabble-rousers, however, knew they were sowing in a field fully prepared for such planting, a hungry field, one with enough water and fertilizer to yield a bountiful crop of opposition to integration. Remember what was at stake here. The white supremacists were not fighting just to preserve the segregation of public schools. They were fighting to preserve a cherished way of life. That this way of life was wrong, immoral, and never should have been propagated in the first place was irrelevant. It had been, it was theirs, and God forbid its associated white privileges be taken from them. Sunday night was their last chance—and they were making the most of it. And then it was Monday morning…

Chapter Twenty-Four

I remember waking up that morning so excited! I changed my mind several times about what to wear, and I think I finally settled on a short-sleeved, white, button-down blouse with a wide collar, and a full cotton skirt which might have been pale blue and gray with a black belt. I'm pretty sure I wore black flats, too, as I remembered I would have to be on the playground at least twice during the day. I probably had a bowl of corn flakes and a cup of coffee, and then I was out the door.

Because it had stormed the night before, the gravel in the driveway was still wet and I could see water droplets on my windshield. Everything looked wet and green as I walked the few steps to my car. The air had a wet-earth-fresh-water smell to it, like after rain has moistened everything and beat all the dust and allergens into the ground. I could hardly wait to get to school and into my classroom.

I knew there had been some demonstrations around Nashville Sunday evening from having watched the news the night before. Most had been in the downtown area and around the schools where some black children had preregistered. Some of the demonstrators had promised picket lines would be set up Monday morning at the elementary schools being desegregated. They strongly encouraged parents to boycott the schools and keep their children home—white parents of course. The parents of black children, on the other hand, had not been "encouraged" to keep their children out of school, they'd been threatened.

I knew a few black first-graders had preregistered at Buena Vista, Glen, Fehr, and some of the other elementary schools, but none had at Hattie Cotton, so I wasn't really expecting much in the way of protesters. I also knew, because she told us, Margaret had been questioned by someone back in August about any black children who might have registered, and she reported none had. When I pulled into the school parking lot I remember looking out towards the street and seeing a few people standing around watching, but there was nothing resembling a crowd or any kind of gathering. Everything appeared to be pretty normal.

I think I got to school at about seven-fifteen, went in the front door, and directly to my classroom. Irene came in shortly after I arrived, and we took a last look at my roster. She tried to give me a few helpful comments about my students, since she knew most of them. I then made sure I had paper, crayons, *and pencils ready, and sat down at my desk to wait for the bell which would tell me it was time to go bring my students in from the playground.*

It was almost surreal. School hadn't even started yet. The first student had not entered my room, but as I sat there a happiness washed over me. I thought about all the anxiety I had felt over the summer from my previous year at McCann. Before the year had ended I was actually wondering if I'd made a mistake going into teaching. And now, here I sat, unreasonably happy, almost giddy with excitement looking around the room and thinking about everything which had brought me to this—my first day at Hattie Cotton. Irene stuck her head in to wish me good luck, and I thanked her again for all she had done to help me get acclimated and settled. She reminded me that I had done a lot of homework on my own to get to this place—it wasn't all her. Still, I am certain I could not have felt more welcome in any school in the country. What a year this was going to be!

Chapter Twenty-Five

By the first day of school Kasper and the crowds around him were in a state of emotional frenzy. Angry and frustrated, they continued trying to breathe life into a dying corpse. The legal decision to end life support for segregation had long since been made. Now the respirator was being unplugged. Their demonstrations may have impacted the turnout for early registration, but they had failed to halt it altogether. The segregationists were desperate. They had done their homework and they had done it well. They knew at which of their schools black children had preregistered and they were out in force. Some of the crowds were large, really large. They were loud, they were intimidating, and they were at times violent. At several of the schools white crowds tried to block the paths of approaching black students and their parents. Police officers, on the order of both Mayor West and the Commissioner, were doing everything possible to try and maintain peace, or at least avoid outright street fights. [43]

Buena Vista had preregistered three black first-graders, and all made it safely to school on their first morning. Things were more tense at the nearby Jones school, where the crowd was bigger and more vocal. Four black children showed up for opening day—three of whom had registered two weeks earlier. None of the children nor their parents were physically attacked, but they did receive incredible amounts of verbal abuse.[44] Had it not been for the presence and efforts of extra police officers, they might never have made it into the building.

Over on Fifth Avenue North, at the Fehr school, things were even more unruly. Four of the five first-graders who had preregistered crossed the segregation line. They had no idea the short tentative steps they were taking into school, as they clutched the hands of their parents, were steps into Tennessee history. One black parent reported that once inside she, her friend, and their children had no trouble at all with any of the teachers or the principal. She even commented how kind some of the white parents had been to them.[45]

---

[43] Egerton
[44] Ibid
[45] Ibid

Such was not the case outside of the school, however. According to one black parent, the women protesting out front, "they were bad." Two of them were eventually arrested and charged with disorderly conduct, while others threw rocks and bottles at the children and their parents as they left the building at noon. Even the black janitor, who had to return to the school mid-afternoon to take down the American flag, was harassed and threatened by a group of white thugs. When he fled back into the school for safety, they slashed the tires on his car.[46]

As bad as conditions were at Buena Vista, Jones, and Fehr, it was across town on the east side of the Cumberland River where the protesters focused most of their attention. The crowds had been strategically organized and urged into action. No black students showed up for the first day of school at Bailey, even though one had preregistered. At Caldwell three black children and their parents met the taunts and jeers of more than a hundred white protesters as they approached the building. The unruly crowd threw rocks, bottles and insults, as they spat upon and cursed both children and adults. A police officer and a black mother were both injured by objects being thrown at them. Another mother, who tried to avoid the crowd by exiting through a side door, was spit on by a group of white youths. Scared to death she fled the school, spittle still on her face.[47]

Glenn School was where Kasper and his followers decided to take their stand. The police had to work hard to keep the crowd of more than two hundred back so the black children could get through. They had gathered early that morning and Kasper did everything he could to whip up anger and furor. Screaming out his vitriol, Kasper admonished the mob, "We've got to defy this thing! They don't have enough jails to hold all of us!" Just before the opening bell three black first graders, Jacqueline Griffith, Lajuanda Street, and Sinclair Lee, Jr., made their way through the riotous gang, up the front walk, and into the school.[48] The intimidation and threatening was strong enough, however, between students who were pulled out and those whose parents just didn't send them, first day attendance was about half of what was expected.

---

[46] Egerton
[47] Ibid
[48] Ibid

Lajuanda Street wasn't intimidated, though, she was just happy and excited to be going to the first grade. She well remembers the crowds on both sides of the street, the hollering and jostling, but she just thought they were having a parade for her. "I thought everybody went to the first grade in a parade,"[49] she remarked.

> *I can remember being so excited! See, my older sister had already gone to school, and she thought she was something special because of it. And now it was my turn. I wore my favorite dress, one my grandma had made, had sown for me. It was a deep purple with a lilac sash and matching bow at the collar. And I wore my best patent leather shoes. I was beyond happy as I held my daddy's hand walking toward the school. I was going to the first grade!*

Her daddy's hand held on tightly to Lajuanda's, because he was a lot less happy and excited than she. He understood the racist terms and the name-calling flying around. He heard the anger in the voices and saw the hate in the eyes of the raucous white crowd. He knew the potential for trouble. In fact, he purposely did not bring Lajuanda's baby sister with them because he knew if they were by themselves and things got bad or dangerous, he could pick up Lajuanda and run. They did make it into the school that morning, but it wasn't without some anxious moments, even if excited six-year-old Lajuanda was oblivious to them.

Emma Clemons and Hattie Cotton schools, also on the east side of Nashville, didn't garner much attention. Clemons, out of an expected enrollment of over five hundred, could possibly have had as many as four black students. None had preregistered, and only one actually went to school the first day: Joy Smith, daughter of the Rev. Kelly Miller Smith, Sr. Rev. Smith received some harassing and threatening phone calls the night before school started, but opening day itself went smoothly for his daughter. When I talked recently with Joy she said,

---

[49] Lajuanda Harley

"You know my parents just didn't make a big deal about it. And I mean, I was six, I had no idea I was the first black child to go to that school. I was just excited to be in the first grade. Looking back on it I know they were concerned, because my father walked me to school for at least the first two weeks, even though it was only a block away. My father was a minister, and I found out later he had stayed late at church the previous night talking with one of the other pastors. I also found out the mayor, Ben West, called him to let him know everything would be all right—so I know they were concerned, but they just didn't make a big deal of it. That first day, I remember I wore my navy-blue sailor dress, and of course we didn't have backpacks in those days, but I had a brand-new book satchel. I remember having my picture taken and some people saying things, but I just figured everyone was excited because I was going to the first grade! It really wasn't until later, weeks, maybe a month, before I realized my presence there could cause some problems."[50]

By the end of the day, though, many of the protesters' goals had been accomplished. Around several of the schools the unruly crowds had been big, and the frenzy strong and intimidating. Classes had been significantly disrupted. Attendance at most schools was way off. The whites who didn't show up mostly stayed away for spite. The blacks who didn't show up, mostly stayed away for safety. The protesters, if they hadn't done anything else, had stirred up a lot of fear and anxiety, enough so that many of the teachers and students who did attend were justifiably scared, and little if anything was accomplished. Yes, the segregationists were feeling pretty good, like the momentum had turned in their favor.[51] At Hattie Cotton, though, opening day appeared to be going well.

---

[50] Joy Smith
[51] Egerton

Chapter Twenty-Six

The next thing I knew, I was jarred back from my daydream by the opening bell. I got up from my desk and headed toward the back of the wing to the playground doors where I was told the children would be waiting for their teachers. I was trying not to look foolishly excited: first day, first opening bell, first students. Could this be real? It was. I got to the door and there they were, lined up just like they were supposed to be: my class in one row and Irene's in another. I introduced myself to the person in front and in we went, almost quietly and almost single file the whole way. All things considered I was pretty impressed—but I didn't tell them that.

When we got to our classroom, I directed them all to their seats using my seating chart, and then asked them to settle down so I could take attendance. Next, I told them to take the small piece of construction paper on their desk, write their name on it, fold it lengthwise like a teepee, and place it in the front left corner of their desk so I could clearly see it. Believe it or not, every single student did as I asked, did it quietly, and in no time it was done—and I could start learning names without having to scan through a book every time I wanted to call on someone. Before I did anything else, I decided I'd tell them a little bit about myself. When I was a student, I had always liked learning things about my teachers, particularly the teachers I liked. I wanted to be one of those teachers.

"As you can see from the chalkboard, my name is Mrs. Bruce, and I'm sure most of you have already figured out I am new here at Hattie Cotton. Last year I taught third grade at McCann Elementary across town, and since Hattie Cotton is much closer to where I live, I am really happy to be here this year. I have heard wonderful things about this school and about all of you, and I am excited about getting to know each one of you. I have no doubt we will have a great year."

And so my tenure at Hattie Cotton began. First, I had everyone take the books out of their desks and we talked briefly about each one and the subject it covered. Then, I believe we did a short writing assignment in their writing books, probably about something they had done over the summer. Before I knew it the recess bell was ringing, and they were all lining up to go outside. Recess is a very big deal in elementary schools!

Once we got out into the hall, Irene caught me to let me know we had in fact had one black child register for first grade that morning, just before the start of school.

"Do you know anything about her?" I asked.

"Just that her name is Patricia Watson, she's six years old, and lives nearby," she responded. "I just heard she and her mother came in about 7:45 this morning, and the mother registered her. She said she would be back to pick her up at noon to take her home. Then she left. That's really all I know."

We were only too aware of what had been going on at some of the other schools in town, so I was a bit concerned. "Do you think everything will be okay here?" I asked. "I didn't see any signs of protesters this morning, did you?"

"No, I didn't notice a thing out of the ordinary."

"Well, let's hope it stays that way, for everyone's sake, but especially for hers, poor kid. I hope the other kids treat her okay." By then we had reached the playground and I looked out at all the laughing, and running, and playing—and for the first time since I'd started, even with all that had been going on around us, I felt a little shiver of concern.

Chapter Twenty-Seven

She had every right to feel concerned. What MaryAnne didn't know, had no way of knowing, was that by the time Irene was filling her in, word of Patricia's arrival had already gotten out and was quickly spreading. She had been registered and put into a first-grade class without any kind of disturbance. Even the general assembly for first graders and their parents went smoothly. It did not appear either Patricia or her mother were treated poorly by anyone, nor shown any signs of disrespect.

It was not long after the little girl arrived, however, before carloads of men began to show up on W. Greenwood Avenue, out in front of the school. Several more cars appeared throughout the morning. As noontime approached, they began to slowly drive around the school. Some of the cars had segregationist banners with racist commentary on them. Others had KKK written on the sides and one could see passengers waving Confederate flags out the windows as they went by. When the 12:00 dismissal time for first graders came there were a number of cars and protesters gathered near the entrance to the school's driveway.[52] Nothing was thrown but you didn't have to listen very hard to hear the foul, racist language.

In addition to what was going on outside, several mothers had come in throughout the morning to quietly withdraw their children. They, too, had heard of Patricia's enrollment and the growing numbers of protesters. Miss Cate actually met with one mother who had come to take her child home, but convinced the woman it really wasn't necessary, and so the child remained. Clearly, though, there was edginess and tension building within the community.

When the half-day was over for the new first graders, the protesters, careful to stay off the school grounds, were almost filling the driveway's entrance. It seemed their belligerence, and bigotry took up more space than their bodies. Most parents came into the school, or up to the front doors to pick up their children. However, when it was time for Patricia's mother to come pick up her daughter, she was so frightened by what was

---

[52] Margaret Cate

going on that she called a taxi to get Patricia and bring her home. When the cab arrived, the crowd of protesters was fairly substantial, and it was drawing courage from its numbers. As the cab tried to make its way into the driveway of the school, the men closed in and began rocking the car, pounding on the hood and trunk. No one was close enough to hear what was said to the driver, but they were finally able to scare him enough so he dared go no further. He just backed up and left.[53]

Inside, Patricia waited for her mother—probably wondering what was taking her so long. When Miss Cate realized Patricia had not been picked up she took her into the office to wait while they figured out what to do. No, Patricia did not know why her mother wasn't there. Neither did she know how to get home from the school. Although some of the details are a bit hazy, it is clear Miss Cate knew what was happening outside. She also knew she was responsible for the safety of the child. So, in order to avoid the possibility of further trouble, she took Patricia by the hand, walked out the main door, crossed the front of the building to where her car was parked, got in and took Patricia home herself. As she was backing out of the driveway, one man actually yelled at her about transporting a Negro child in her car, but Miss Cate, with no regard to personal danger, did what she had to do—she took care of her student.[54]

We know, too, that when Margaret got Patricia home, she asked her mother why she hadn't arranged for her to get home after school. She discovered the woman had been frightened enough by the protesting, she had called for a taxi to pick Patricia up at noon. Margaret recalled having seen a taxi out front at one point and surmised the rest. She apologized for all the disturbance, said her goodbyes, and returned to school to finish out her day.[55]

We humans are often quick to toss out the cliché when we perceive someone's talk is more evident than their walk. But that day, Margaret Cate embodied everything MaryAnne had learned about her. She exemplified her duty as a principal. She braved her beliefs as a human being. And while she may not have talked about her faith, that day she certainly walked it.

---

[53] Margaret Cate
[54] Ibid
[55] Ibid

Chapter Twenty-Eight

Once we came in from recess, we spent the rest of the morning doing "get acquainted" kinds of things, mostly to help me get acquainted with them—since most of them already knew each other. I had this game that was very easy for them and very helpful to me. I had them all line up around the room. The first one would say, for example, "My name is Sue Ellen and I like fried okra." The next person would say, Sue Ellen likes fried okra; my name is Bobby and I like caramel pie." And the next one would say, "Sue Ellen likes fried okra, Bobby likes caramel pie; my name is Linda and I like barbeque," and so forth and so on. By the time we got around the whole class, I probably had about seventy-five percent of them down pat. It aggravates me to death that out of all of them, I can remember so few names. Today, the only one I can really say I remember is Dixie. I definitely remember I had a girl named Dixie.

At noon I took the class to the lunchroom. Some of the kids bought hot lunches while others had brought their own bag lunches from home. They weren't wild, but the lunchroom was pretty noisy with my class, Irene's, and the two fifth-grade classes all in there together. Fortunately, most of the kids were hungry and focused on eating—or talking with their friends. By then the teachers had heard, and some of us had glimpsed, what was going on out front, but in those days we sat and ate lunch with our classes, so we did our best to keep them occupied and blissfully unaware of the activity out on Greenwood. When we had finished eating we lined up again to go outside for noon recess. We walked back by our classroom so anybody with a lunchbox could drop it off and then made our way out to the playground.

While we were outside Irene filled me in on the few details she had picked up about little Patricia Watson, Miss Cate having to bring her home, and the protesters out front. Even though there hadn't been any real violence, their presence was unnerving, a little scary actually. They seemed determined to try and make trouble. We talked a little about the whole integration issue and how sad it was that kids were having to experience all the ugliness associated with it. We both knew kids just wanted to be kids and left to their own devices; they didn't care a fig about what color they were. It was adults who were causing all the turmoil. I prayed they would all just go home and leave us alone.

By the time classes were over teachers had received word we were not to stay too long after school. A police officer had been assigned to patrol out front, but we should make our way out of the building while he was still around—just in case. When I left it was raining and things had pretty much quieted down—I think I recall seeing a few people milling around under the trees across the street, but that was about it. I can remember feeling badly for Patricia, embarrassed really, and I didn't even know her, had never met her, but she was just a little child. I also remember feeling a slight sense of relief, somewhat thankful it all hadn't been worse. I hoped people would begin to come to their senses, and the next day would be calmer.

Chapter Twenty-Nine

Tragically, MaryAnne's feelings of relief that "it could have been worse" were premature, because that night it got worse—much worse. It seemed there was no way to calm people down and stem the fury. The anger and resentment continued to build in direct proportion to the feelings of desperation which increased with every passing hour.

Kasper and his lackeys were busy trying to build and maintain riot status around the State Capital. The first day of integration was accomplished, but there was no way Kasper was going to give up. With a rope in hand, he was literally trying to whip up the fury of his hundreds-strong crowd. A few minutes later, after having shouted, "let's show them what a white man can do," there was an effigy of a black man swinging from a traffic light on Church Street, with a sign around it reading "This could be you!"[56] Meanwhile, things were getting even more vicious north of the city.

While the Kasper crowd was taking care of business downtown, another mob was engaged in greater mischief and mayhem to the north. Under the cloak of darkness, a mob, estimated to be between four and five hundred, was moving around the streets in the area of Fehr Elementary School, which had also been desegregated that morning, one of the black students being Grace McKinley's daughter, Linda. As the darkness increased so did the mob's energy and daring and violence. Suddenly, and without warning, two outbuildings in the back yard of Grace McKinley's Sixth Avenue home burst into flames. Burning crosses appeared outside the houses of several black families who lived in the area. There was also some talk about Fehr being blown up at midnight. Rocks were thrown at cars with Negro occupants. Additional homes and other properties were vandalized. All of this happened within a few crazy minutes, and then the cowards were gone, disappearing by the time the police arrived.[57] But even that mob action was not the worst.

---

[56] Egerton
[57] Ibid

Midnight, September 10, 1957 had just passed. Rain was falling as police officer Joe Casey arrived at his East Nashville home after completing his shift patrolling the streets around Fehr School. Things had been reasonably quiet. As soon as he entered his house, Casey safely put away his gun and holster and was heading toward his kitchen when a powerful explosion rocked the area with such force windows were blown out in nearby houses. The blast was felt as far away as Donelson. Officer Casey, not a small man, who lived about a block from the explosion on West McKennie Avenue was literally knocked off his feet and thrown against the far wall of his living room. Recovering himself quickly, he grabbed his gun and headed back out the door. A billowing cloud of thick, acrid smoke told Casey in which direction to head, though he likely already knew.[58] Seconds later as he arrived at 1033 West Greenwood Avenue, Casey could see a significant part of the school had been severely damaged. What was once the school's entrance area, library, and infirmary was now a mass of twisted metal, broken glass, dangling ceiling tiles, and huge piles of brick and rubble. No one could have created a more obscene picture than was the Hattie Cotton School at that moment.

---

[58] Egerton

Chapter Thirty

My mind was still in one of those cottony states when I answered the phone at about 5:00 the next morning, so much so it took a few seconds for me to realize it was someone from the superintendent's office calling. I have no idea all these years later who it was, but I well remember what it was about: my school had been torn apart by a dynamite blast. According to the caller, I was to report to school at the regular time and someone would be there to direct us where to wait. I hung up and started toward the television, but before I could get there the phone rang again. Surely I would now discover this was just a bad dream and the new caller would wake me up or tell me it was all a mistake. But it was Irene, calling to make sure I had heard and see if I was okay. Okay? Oh my God, how could I possibly be okay? I thanked her for calling and said I'd see her at school in a couple of hours. At that point, as I headed toward the living room to turn on the television set, I wasn't even sure if there was a school left.

I thought the TV set would never warm up after I'd flipped the knob. And then, there it was, the most wretched scene I had ever witnessed in my life: Hattie Cotton School, my school, blown to pieces. I remember immediately praying no one had been hurt, or worse yet, killed. Then I started to feel sick. Then I started to cry as I thought, "My students will be devastated. I'm devastated." Next came the horror, the disbelief, the shock. Shortly thereafter the anger, pain, and nausea kicked in—and then more anger. Children—it was a place for children for God's sake! Why would anyone destroy a place for children?

As I looked at the news footage, I began piecing things together as much as my muddled brain would let me. It couldn't be real. It wasn't real. But there it was, on my little twelve-inch black and white television, beating me in the face better than any bully ever could. My soul was bloodied even if my nose wasn't. The tears were falling. It must be some other place, some other school, Little Rock maybe, or Atlanta, or Birmingham. But I knew it wasn't. I recognized the shrubs that were still there and the brick façade beyond the blown-out section. I could reconstruct the twisted metal window frames, and they fit into place in my memory. What was happening to my world, to my school, to its community, to its students…my students? How could I bear getting ready and going there? But I had to. I had been directed to. Even if I hadn't, I *had to go: for Miss Cate, for Irene, for my students. And so, at about 6:00 a.m., I tore myself away from the hypnotizing images, left the TV on with the volume turned up, and went to get ready…for school.*

Chapter Thirty-One

It wasn't long before Officer Casey, first on the scene, was joined by Sargent John Wise. Almost immediately he radioed police headquarters to say they needed to seal off all roads leading to and from Hattie Cotton School. Children and parents, literally shaken from their sleep, some still in their bedclothes, were already showing up in droves to see what had happened. The adults, shocked and horrified at what they were seeing, tried to comfort their kids, many of whom were in tears as they gazed with disbelief into the jagged, unnatural cavern which the day before had been their library. Casey and Wise did their best to keep people back from the building until additional police officers and the fire department arrived to clear the blast area and rope off the school.[59]

Within about a half an hour, Police Chief Hosse appeared on the scene, the strong smell of dynamite still in the blown-out wing, the acrid smoke and dust still hanging in the air. The Chief, who earlier in the evening had received a call from Mayor West praising him for having gotten through the day with no bloodshed, was disbelieving at what he saw. There was still no bloodshed, but the destruction was great. Hosse issued a statement saying efforts to maintain peace would be doubled, and "every man will be available to protect the schools."[60] Police Sargent Robert Justice picked up a clock as he took a cursory look through the wreckage. Except for a broken frame it was still intact, telling him the blast, which had ripped it from its hanging place, demolishing the wall and severing its electrical connection, had occurred at precisely 12:33 a.m.[61]

Looking at the horrific scene, if there was anything to be thankful for it was that the blast could have been even worse. Thank God no one was killed. Had the dynamite been placed further toward the center of the building than toward the west corner, it is likely more classrooms would have been damaged or destroyed, and more children displaced. Not that the damage was limited, for it was extensive. Still, it could have been even worse.

---

[59] "Blast Wrecks School."
[60] Ibid.
[61] Ibid.

How sad, how tragic, merely thirty minutes into a new day and a large part of a nearly new school, was heavily damaged. The ugly, gaping hole in the building could not compare to the hole in the hearts of the onlookers or the soul of the community. I suspect you could feel the horror of the neighborhood residents as they stared at the destruction. I suspect, too, you could almost hear the frustrated and frightened questions many of them were surely asking themselves, perhaps even each other. Why? How do they think this can be helping them? Is this worth it? Is this really what they want? My question back to them would have been: Who is they?

Chapter Thirty-Two

I don't think I ate breakfast or even had a cup of coffee before I left the house that morning. I just recall feeling sick, physically sick. After I tore my eyes away from the television, I had to force myself to get dressed, walk out to the car, get in it, and start it up. I was doing everything in slow motion, including driving into Nashville. I must have thought the longer I could delay getting to school the longer I could pretend the nightmare wasn't happening, or at least things weren't as bad as they looked on TV. There weren't many traffic lights between my house and Hattie Cotton in those days, but I remember hoping every one of them would be red.

It wasn't long, though, certainly not long enough, before I was making my right-hand turn onto Greenwood Avenue from Gallatin Pike. I had not gone far before I reached the point where the road was blocked off. A police officer approached my car to say I could not drive any further. I explained I was a teacher at Hattie Cotton, and he told me I would need to park and walk the rest of the way, which I did.

Now I was back to forcing myself. I almost couldn't tell if I was actually conscious or hallucinating. It took willpower I didn't realize I had just to put one foot in front of the other to make it the few hundred feet up to the school. Looking ahead I could see a blurry crowd of people. I could begin to hear voices, and before long the blur started coming into focus. My stomach was on the verge of nausea and my head was pounding. This could not be happening, and yet everything my disbelieving eyes were taking in showed me it was. There was this odd smell hovering in the air, like a mixture of damp earth, gun powder, and fear. Never before and never since had such a short walk taken so much out of me. Never had I so badly wanted to just give up and collapse.

I finally cleared the last house on my right and the east end of the school was coming into view. As I continued walking up Greenwood Avenue, more and more of the building entered my peripheral vision. I could see the trees at the east corner, more of the building, the shrubbery in front of it. A little more, and a little more still. Then, finally I had gone far enough I could no longer avoid it. I was across the street from the school's driveway, and I had to see the angry, gruesome sight. I had to look past the twisted, shattered, and broken exterior into this awful abyss that a few hours ago had been a modern school library, which existed for the sole purpose of educating and enlightening young *minds, to help them grow and develop into good people so they were equipped to help make the world a better place.*

Somewhere I remember hearing a saying, one I'm not sure meant too much to me at the time. It went something like, "once you look at something, once you see it, you can't ever again really 'unsee' it." It meant something to me then, when I had to look at...I had to see...the face of hatred.

Chapter Thirty-Three

As bad as things were for MaryAnne and her fellow teachers, imagine for a minute, if you can, what it must have been like to be Margaret Cate. Already she had been subject to criticism for allowing a Negro child into the school. She had been admonished for transporting a Negro child, a six-year-old little girl, who had no other way to get home from school. And now, a significant part of the school was a pile of rubble, and sections which had not been destroyed were, for the time being, rendered unusable. Try for a minute to imagine that.

By all accounts—newspaper articles, personal letters from students, friends and admirers, stories from her nephew, George—Margaret Cate was an incredible woman. She had dedicated her life to others in a variety of ways. She understood being in service to other people…life just doesn't get any better. Through public education as both a teacher and administrator, through her church where she taught Sunday school for years, through her writing of plays, newsletters, articles, even a novel, Miss Cate deeply touched people of all ages. Clearly, her life's goal was helping them build better, fuller, more spiritual, more informed lives.[62]

Having moved to Nashville from Kentucky at the age of twenty, when her father died, Cate earned both a bachelor's degree in education and a master's degree in history from Peabody College. She began her career in public education at Central High School, Nashville, in 1928, while still a student herself.[63] Every passing year had helped Margaret build an impressive resume and reputation, It doesn't take much research, however, to realize Margaret Cate was far more concerned with building up other people than in building her own career.

Miss Cate was assigned as principal of the Hattie Cotton School when it opened in 1950 and was loved and respected by both her students and her faculty. She worked long hours, and it was well known she did much if not most of her administrative duties before and after the school

---

[62] Jack Bond. "Account Of Birth Of Christ."
[63] Michael Cass. "Margaret R. Cate."

day. Why? Because if she were doing administrative things during school, she couldn't be visiting classrooms. And if she couldn't be in classrooms, well, there's no telling how many stories, games, poetry recitations, or student presentations she might have missed.

That is but a small piece of the Margaret Cate who now had to deal with the likes of, not a misbehaving student, not an upset staff member, not even an irate parent, but a terrorist. This was no protest or rally. It wasn't just some frustrated racist spewing a nasty comment about her transporting a Negro child. This was a bombing! This was somebody, or probably somebodies, who brought hate and venom to her doorstep, who tried to destroy a building which was her second home, that represented and housed much of what she loved, valued, held dear, and revered in life.

Now imagine, if you can, how Miss Cate felt when, presumably unbeknownst to anyone else, she answered a phone call on the afternoon of the first day of school. The caller wanted to make her aware of a group of people trying to convince parents to keep their children home the next day. Or how she might have felt later in the evening when she answered another call at home, again taking her to task for transporting a Negro child. Or how she must have felt at 6:30 the next morning when she received yet another anonymous call from a woman who spit into the phone, "You won't be carrying any nigger child home now, will you?" and then slammed down the receiver.[64] Just imagine…if you can.

---

[64] Margaret Cate

Rev. Fred Stroud leading protestors outside of Glenn School

Car being readied for protest parade

Demonstrator shouting from traffic light post

Segregationists protest

Protestors on street at Glenn School

Car at segregationist rally

Crowd protesting outside Glenn School

John Kasper leading protestors at Glenn School

Crowd lines street at Fehr School

Harassed by protestors, Grace McKinley taking Rita Buchanan and Linda McKinley to school

Parents walk child to Fehr School

Mother taking daughter to Buena Vista School

Parents taking child to Fehr School

Protestors at Fehr School

Policeman escorting blacks to Fehr School

Registration day at Glenn School

Marvin Moore's first day at Nashville's Jones Elementary School in 1957.

Children arriving at Hattie Cotton School

Lajuanda Street attending Glenn School

One of Nashville's first integrated classrooms in September, 1957.

The Nashville Banner *newspaper from Tuesday, September 10, 1957. Used by permission.*

Hattie Cotton School following bombing

Hatie Cotton School undergoing repairs

Hattie Cotton School Library

Officials examine damage

Officials with Mayor West survey damage

Official holds clock showing exact time of blast

Damaged classroom

Protestor arrested

John Kasper arrested

Protestor arrested

Officials examine evidence

Nashville police making arrests

Nashville police

Nashville police making arrests

Nashville police presence at protest

Car used in parades by KKK

(Top) Irene Spivey (right) and MaryAnne Bruce (second from right) and other staff prepare for start of school

Patricia Watson, who attended Hattie Cotton school on September 9, 1957, and never returned. She died on May 5, 2020. (Photograph provided by her granddaughter, Lenora Cassell.)

Chapter Thirty-Four

Having to look at the destruction was almost more than I could bear. Monday morning I had been so excited I could hardly stand it. A mere twenty-four hours later I was so distraught I couldn't stand it. Shock, disbelief, anguish, call it what you will—I was an emotional wreck. The police had cordoned off the area so there weren't a lot of students or parents close by, but my colleagues were here. We were crying, hugging, trying to talk, attempting to make some sort of sense out of the insanity at which we could not stop looking. It was like one of those accident scenes where the sight almost makes you sick, yet you still can't look away.

While my eyes were almost in a hypnotic state of staring, my mind kept thinking about all the time I had spent over the previous two weeks getting ready for school to start. I thought about touring the school with Miss Cate and about learning where all the supplies were kept from Irene. I thought about all the lesson plans she had shared with me, and how I had planned to use some of them and adapt others to my personality. Can you believe it, I remember thinking about the stupid ditto machine and wondering if it was in a billion pieces, and if the whole area around the teacher's room smelled like duplicator fluid. I thought about my decorated classroom walls and the bulletin boards and my name on the chalkboard. I wondered if any of it was still there. I wondered if the walls were even still standing.

Because I was so new, I really didn't even know a lot of the faculty— pretty much just Irene and Miss Cate. So mostly I stood and fought tears, and mostly I lost the battle. I thought about who might have done this horrible thing and if they would be caught. I wondered if it was that fool John Kasper. I wondered if whoever had done it was feeling some kind of smug satisfaction, or if maybe they regretted it and were feeling remorse. I wondered how sick an individual must have to be to think something like this could ever be justified. I am not a violent person, but I wanted those responsible to feel pain, the kind of pain they had inflicted on all of us.

And every time I thought about my pain, I thought about my students, and the pain they must be feeling, or would feel when they saw what had happened to their school. At some point during the morning, I remember two of my friends from college came by, Bob Stroud (no relation to Rev. John Stroud) and his girlfriend Betsy Adams, just to show their moral support. I had talked *with them right before school started to tell them about my assignment to Hattie Cotton School and how excited I was about the fresh start. They saw the news reports on TV, remembered I was there, and because they knew me so well, they also knew how devastated I would be.*

The TV might have told them what was going on, but it was God who sent them. For just a few moments I was able to collapse into someone's arms—and I needed to collapse. We hugged, shared a few tears and, looking at the wreckage in front of us, talked about the tragedy—not just in terms of the damaged building, but the damaged lives, possibly damaged forever, scarred deeply by the trauma. I remember while we were talking, I kept thinking about Patricia Watson and wondering if she was okay, wondering what she was feeling, the lasting scars she must have. I wondered if we would ever see her again.

Chapter Thirty-Five

I kept thinking about Patricia, too, throughout much of MaryAnne's story. At least as much as Patricia, who was after all only six years old, I kept thinking about her mother, Ms. Ernestine Watson Baugh. I thought about her in much the same way I thought about Margaret Cate: Imagine what it must have been like to be Mrs. Baugh. Imagine her life at 7:45 a.m. on September 9, 1957, and then just four hours later—and all the hours, days, months, and years that followed.

Surely Mrs. Baugh felt a bit anxious when she left Patricia in the hands of a white teacher and a white principal, in a school where every single one of the other 392 students were white, where there had never been a black student before. I'm pretty sure it would have made me a bit anxious. The entire process, however, went off essentially without incident, so maybe she left a bit less nervous than when she arrived. But then, presumably, to start out her door a few hours later to pick Patricia up from the first day at her new school…imagine what that must have been like.

Although we have no way of knowing for sure, it is likely Mrs. Baugh walked out of her house and headed north, up McFerrin Ave. toward W. Greenwood. I doubt she would have gotten very far up W. Greenwood before she would have seen cars with racist placards or Confederate flags and sensed what was happening. It's possible someone had alerted her about the demonstration going on, and therefore she never left her house. No matter how she found out, try to imagine the terror she must have felt: Lord have mercy, what is happening? My little girl, my Patricia! What have I done? What am I going to do? Think about what it would be like to be a mother who suddenly realizes she has placed her child, her flesh and blood, in harm's way, very possibly in serious harm's way.

Mrs. Baugh is quoted as having said she was too afraid to walk back to the school to get Patricia. I strongly suspect she was far more frightened for the safety of her daughter than for herself. And if she were accosted or attacked on the way into the school, what would happen to Patricia then? It makes a great deal of sense she would have called for a cab to pick up Patricia once she realized what was happening around the school. It certainly would have been safer for both her and her daughter than trying to make it on foot through an angry, racist mob, that might do, say, or throw most anything. And of course, there would be no way for her to know the taxi driver never made it.

Now can you imagine the overwhelming flood of relief Mrs. Baugh must have felt when she looked out her window and saw Patricia and the principal getting out of a car, and the panic that would have been quelled seeing her daughter, unharmed, come in the front door? Think about it. One must assume Mrs. Baugh wanted her daughter to have the best education possible, and to be as close to home as possible. Hattie Cotton was only a few blocks away. It was a fairly new school. It had an excellent reputation, wonderful leadership, and an outstanding faculty. These things were obviously not secrets—MaryAnne had discovered all of them and more just from talking to people. What parents wouldn't want this kind of school for their child? And so, even with all of the protests going on around the city, which may very well be why Patricia was not preregistered, Mrs. Baugh was willing to run the risk so her daughter could get every educational advantage available.

Then imagine what Mrs. Baugh must have felt when she was jolted from bed later that night, possibly knocked out of her bed. I wonder how long it took her to realize what had happened. I doubt it took long. She might have even sensed it immediately. Imagine all that must have been going through her mind as the shaking sensation and the noise of the blast was replaced by the sounds of fire and police sirens. The wondering would have been replaced by the first shudder of realization, which would have evolved quickly to fear, and then even more quickly to outright panic. It could not have been long before Mrs. Baugh realized Hattie Cotton had been blown up because of her child. She may have even suspected it wouldn't have made much difference to the bombers if Patricia had actually been in the building when it blew. She may not have been the literal target, but Patricia certainly could be seen as the cause. For this family, there was no way to come out of the ordeal whole, no way to "get past it" or "move on." Now can you imagine why Patricia never went back? I sure can.

Chapter Thirty-Six

There are so many details about that day, and the rest of the week, which escape me. I know the fire department and city engineers were trying to establish the safety and integrity of the structure before allowing anyone in. I think I recall some of the neighbors offering us water or iced tea. They may also have offered us snacks and use of their bathrooms, but I'm not certain. I do remember sometime in the early afternoon, with a fireman escorting us, we were allowed into the building to get any of our personal things we might have left there or things we might need when we started teaching again, whenever and wherever that might be. I knew how difficult it would be, but I also knew I had to go in. I had to get some of my things, and I had to see what was still intact—as well as what had been damaged. Walking around to the back of the building was almost as difficult as walking up Greenwood Avenue had been earlier that morning.

Once more, my stomach churned and I was feeling sick. I was thinking about my students and how glad I was they couldn't see their school like this, how glad I was they couldn't see me like this. Yesterday morning we had all been so happy, so excited to start a new year. I had walked into the building with my feet barely touching the ground I was so thrilled. Now, I was having to be vigilant as we walked, trying to avoid shards of glass and hunks of bricks and concrete which had flown well outside of the wrecked building, stepping carefully so as not to stumble or twist an ankle. We walked around jagged portions of doors and doorframes, pieces of chairs and desks and books and…it's a wonder I didn't break my neck. My eyes were seeing all the destruction, there was no way to block it out, but my mind was way more focused on the fear of my destination than on the obstacles to getting there.

Finally, we arrived at the back of our fifth and sixth grade wing. It was far enough from the blast, so while the glass was all blown out, the door itself was still mostly in one piece, unlike my heart, which was breaking into dozens of pieces. I distinctly remember stepping through the open door to my room from the hall. I couldn't tell you if someone had opened it before I got there or if it was blown off, but what assaulted me as I stepped in…is something I definitely can tell you. Almost every piece of furniture in the room had been blown back against the end wall, the farthest most point in the room from where the dynamite had gone off. Chairs on top of desks on top of more chairs, *some tipped over, some right side up, still others upside down. At first it looked like the room had been ransacked by crazy people, and lots of them. Then I began to notice all the loose floor tiles and slabs of concrete that had buckled up, and the ceiling tiles lying in pieces on the floor along with big chunks of the brick walls. And there were pieces of glass everywhere. No, actually the room looked exactly like what had happened, like a bomb had gone off. I just stood there for several seconds, tears straining for release, trying to breath without hyperventilating, trying not to completely fall apart.*

Chapter Thirty-Seven

While MaryAnne and the other teachers spent the day at Hattie Cotton, agonizing over the destruction, the press was busy reporting on it, and the police were busy looking for those who caused it. Almost as soon as he was awakened to the report of the blast, Chief Hosse put out the order for John Kasper to be picked up. During the morning briefing to his patrolmen the chief noted, "this has gotten beyond integration. These people who are following Kasper around have turned violent, blowing up our schools, destroying our property." He admonished his officers they had a job to do, and no matter who was violating them, the laws had to be enforced. By 9:00 a.m. Kasper had been almost ripped out of bed by police and brought in for questioning. A number of other suspects had also been picked up for interrogation regarding the bombing.[65]

Determined to keep students and parents safe, as well as the school buildings, police set up roadblocks and barricades around every desegregated school in the city. Caldwell School is where the police encountered their most forceful resistance from the crowds, who evidently thought the bombing had given them some momentum. They would soon discover the momentum was now shifting to the authorities, and the more moderate, law-abiding citizens, and away from the segregationists and white supremacists. When the protesters pushed up against the barricades and got rowdy the police surrounded them. Those who got too aggressive found themselves in cuffs and thrown into a waiting paddy wagon, much to the shock and dismay of the other protesters. The police were done with passive accommodation. They had a mandate to maintain law and order, and they meant to do so.[66]

As the day after the explosion wore on, it became increasingly clear the bombing had not accomplish its desired effect. Rather than deal a death blow to integration, by fanning the flames of fear and discontent, it dealt a death blow to the opposition, by underscoring the cost of hatred. No little Negro child had caused this destruction. No group of Negro children

---

[65] Egerton
[66] Ibid

had, nor had those children's parents. No, this destruction was caused by diehard racists. It was caused by hate. It was caused by white supremacists. The radicals had been able to pull in some of the mainstream citizenry, the semi-bigots or bigots lite, when it was mostly talk and a few rocks and bottles tossed at the blacks. But dynamite? Blowing up a school? That crossed a line even some of the hard-core segregationists wouldn't step over. Conservative publisher of The Nashville Banner, James Stahlman, thrashed Kasper in an editorial in the afternoon edition of his paper, calling him "a lawless renegade interloper" and "an uninvited evangel of mischief [who] has sown the malevolent seed for this harvest of terrorism." In addition, he offered a $1,000 reward for information about and prosecution of the bombers. Even the all-white, segregationist TFCG was distancing itself from the violence, and from John Kasper, with whom they had worked closely the previous weeks.[67]

Tuesday morning saw the police doubling down on crowd control, arresting anyone who threatened to disturb a smooth peaceful start to the school day. Sadly, attendance was off, and would remain so for the rest of the week, but there was no alteration or modification to the integration plan or the operation of the schools, save for the obvious disruption at Hattie Cotton. At Jones School Barbara Jean Watson, Marvin Moore, Charles Battles, and Cecil Ray Jr. all returned the next morning, as did Erroll Groves and Ethel Mai Carr to Buena Vista, where they would continue attending through the sixth grade. Five of the six who integrated Fehr transferred out leaving only Linda Gail McKinley, who remained for four years.[68]

At Clemons School, Joy Smith was back on the 10th, and there she would remain through grade six, but it was years before she was not the only black student in her class. She recalled her parents were concerned after the bombing, and there was some discussion about her staying home the next day. "But," she went on, "there really wasn't much question I would go. I think my father walked me to school for at least the first two

---

[67] Egerton
[68] Ibid

weeks, even though we only lived about a block away, but there was no way I wasn't going to school."[69] And it was much the same for Lauanda Street, who went back the next day and stayed for the entire year. In fact, she claims, "I really had a good time in school, and had almost no negative experiences."[70]

But the story was certainly different at Hattie Cotton the next day. The only children there, most with their parents, were outside of the building looking in, many crying, devastated at what had been done to their school. The only lessons being taught there were visual lessons, real life lessons—in the consequences of blind rage and unchecked fury, and in the incredible power of hate. It was a lesson Shakespeare had tried to teach a few centuries before, when hatred born of a longstanding feud between the Montagues and Capulets destroyed the lives of their two youngest children. It was a lesson the Bible taught millennia before, in the story of Cain and Abel.

This, however, was not a fictional play being performed at the Globe Theater. It wasn't a Bible story taught in Sunday school or church. This was the here and now. This was real. This lesson was one Mamie Till wanted us to learn a few years before when she provided the photographs of her son's ravaged and brutalized body. Will we never learn? Will we ever realize hate never builds anything good, that hate only destroys? That Tuesday morning, one ten-year-old boy, while staring at the tragic sight of his school remarked, "It makes me real sick inside."[71] I have no doubt it did—him and many others.

[69] Joy Smith
[70] Lajuanda Harley
[71] *The Nashville Tennessean*

Chapter Thirty-Eight

I stood just inside the doorway for several seconds, almost hypnotized by the scene before me, like I was seeing everything through some sort of semi-conscious, altered state. I remember realizing, even with the mask they had given me, it was hard to breath and my eyes were burning from all the dust. Then the fireman who had escorted me in brought me back to reality: "We've cleared a way to your desk Mrs. Bruce. If you can get any of your personal things, you really shouldn't stay in here any longer than necessary. We think this section of the building is structurally okay, but the air is pretty bad." I nodded my understanding.

Slowly and carefully I made my way through the chaos to my desk. Miraculously the two framed pictures I had on top of it were still there—or maybe the fireman had picked them up and placed them there—one of my mother and father and another of my husband and me. I placed them in the satchel I had brought. I also found the lesson plans I had written for the week and my attendance register, both of which were in the top drawer of my desk. As I pushed the drawer closed, I remember wondering if I would ever put anything in it again. As a second thought I checked to be sure the other drawers didn't have anything I needed and thank God I did. In the bottom drawer was my Children's Lit anthology. I grabbed it, knowing I would want to use it. I didn't know then just how instrumental it would be in helping my class through the next several months.

As I headed back to the door, I noticed most of my calendar was gone, that section of wall having been damaged by the blast. I remember sadly thinking I wouldn't need it now anyway. My gaze then moved around and I saw my "Student Work" sign on the opposite wall, which was less damaged. It made me even sadder, knowing no papers would be taped up there, at least not anytime soon. Some pieces of the alphabet chart were still in place, but most were hanging askew or had been blown down by the blast wave. All my work to get the room ready for the first day of school, to make it a place where my students would feel comfortable, a place where they'd feel like they belonged, and in an instant was all shattered. As I wallowed in my own self-pity, I thought about all the other teachers in the school who had done many of the same things to their rooms I had done to mine. They were surely feeling the *same way I was—none of us knowing when or if we would ever be back in our rooms.*

That might have been when it really hit me, even harder than it did looking at the building from the outside. All of this horror, wreckage, and destruction was grounded in hatred, in pure, racist hatred. Destroying a school, a place for children. How can people hate enough to do such a thing? One little girl, a six-year-old child. How could anyone hate that much?

When I got outside, I looked over to my left, toward the other two wings, and could see the damage was not as extensive in those areas of the building. The playground wasn't damaged as much either. I guess there were some things to be thankful for. I wondered when the other grades might get back into the building and when the playground would have kids on it again. I wondered if little Patricia would ever come back. For different reasons, the walk away from the school was every bit as sad and depressing as the walk into it had been. I remember thinking in a few seconds Hattie Cotton had seen enough hate to last a lifetime, and I resolved to do everything in my power, to use every ounce of training I'd had and every bit of humanity I possessed to show my students nothing but love. No matter where we ended up, no matter how long it took to get there, and no matter how long it took us to get back here, hate was not going to win.

Chapter Thirty-Nine

A lthough things were tense for the teachers at virtually all the elementary schools in Nashville the day after the bombing, and especially crazy for those at Hattie Cotton, the police department and the judiciary were on overdrive. Judges were issuing search warrants, police officers were making arrests as fast as they could round up suspects, district attorneys were filing charges, and a grand jury was empaneled. The public wanted answers and law enforcement wanted to provide them. Most of the charges being filed, however, were for disorderly conduct, inciting to riot, disturbing the peace, criminal threatening, and the like. So far, nobody had been charged in the actual bombing of Hattie Cotton.

The next day one nearby resident told a reporter her first thought, after almost being thrown from her bed by the blast, was, "Oh my God! Just think what this would have been if the children had been in the classroom!"[72] Even in the wing furthest from the blast site, it is doubtful they would have survived. What if someone had been walking by the school when the blast went off, or maybe cutting through the school yard on their way home? In many of the nearby houses, particularly those just across the street from the school, if someone had simply been looking out a window they could have been seriously injured or even killed. People definitely wanted those responsible caught and punished. When crimes went unsolved it just compounded the insult. It was like the criminals won, justice was not being served, and was unacceptable.

Of course, everyone knew who was responsible, they just couldn't prove it. And there is a vast difference between what you know intellectually and what you can prove legally. In the ensuing hours and days many people were picked up, questioned, and in some cases even charged, but not with the bombing. Investigators found evidence of a blasting cap on the scene. They matched some electrical wires found in the trunk of a car, one seen speeding away from the school, to pieces found in the blast area. They

---

[72] "Blast Wrecks School"

also investigated a story from an alleged accomplice about a stolen case of dynamite from a construction which site in Franklin, Tennessee.[73] Still, with all the evidence they had, most of it was circumstantial, not conclusive enough to result in an arrest.

There was enough evidence, though, to prompt police and school officials to file a request with the court for an Order of Protection against John Kasper, Fred Stroud, and several others. Kasper, in particular, had made enough enemies that within twenty-four hours of the attack on Hattie Cotton School he was arrested three times. Each time he made bail he was arrested on another charge. Folks in law enforcement had evidently decided they were done playing Kasper's game. Now it was time to play their own. And their game plan was to keep him locked up and off the streets in any way possible for as long as possible.[74] They didn't have enough to charge him in the bombing, but they had enough to put him behind bars for a while—and they did.

---

[73] Egerton
[74] Ibid

PART THREE
(Hattie Cotton Elementary/East High School)

Of all the teachings, beliefs, and aphorisms Morrie
Schwartz shared with us, this is the most
important of all: Love is the only rational act.

—Mitch Albom, *Tuesdays with Morrie*

Love and compassion are necessities, not luxuries.
Without them humanity cannot survive.

—Dalai Lama

Chapter Forty

One of the byproducts of a great tragedy is it can often bring people together, rally the human spirit, inspire goodness. The bombing had brought out the worst in some, but it also brought out the best in many others. With a lot of hard work, and the strong, steady leadership of Margaret Cate, nine of Cotton's thirteen classrooms were ready to receive their students just one week later, including the first grade. Sadly, Patricia Watson was not one of those students who returned to Hattie Cotton on September 17, 1957—nor would she ever.

While the speedy repairs were being made to Hattie Cotton School, work was also underway at the superintendent's office, as the search was on for a place where the fifth and sixth grades could hold classes for the next several months. It was the wing, behind the library, which had been damaged the worst. The temporary space needed to be large enough to accommodate two classes of twenty-five each, and it needed to be in the East Nashville area, so as not to create a major transportation problem for parents.

It didn't take long before a workable solution was found. Assistant Superintendent Oliver, who was also the principal at East High School, came to the rescue. While the repairs, renovations, and clean up were going on at Hattie Cotton, similar activities were happening a few blocks away at East High. With a little skilled carpentry, a lot of general labor, and a dose or two of creativity MaryAnne and Irene had an interim home, a short-term one they hoped. By the time grades one through four moved back into their repaired classrooms on the 17th of September, MaryAnne, Irene, and their gaggle of sixth graders moved into theirs as well.

The temporary classrooms turned out to be a hastily converted storage room for band instruments on the top floor of East High School a few blocks over on Gallatin Pike. Tubas and baritones, flutes and piccolos, tympani, snares, and cymbals, including all the cases, were removed to make way for classroom furnishings and children. Shelving, cabinets, and storage closets were ripped out. The walls were then patched to cover the exposed nail and screw holes. Once the room was empty, the floors were stripped, waxed, and sealed. Desks and chairs were brought in, along with a couple of small rolling chalkboards. In less than a week the closet was transformed into a classroom, two classrooms actually.

It was far from a perfect solution to be sure, considering it was over a half mile from Hattie Cotton, not to mention up three flights of stairs from where they entered the building. But, it was functional nonetheless, and it was a place to "be." It was a place where MaryAnne and Irene could try to rebuild a sense of safety and security for their students, to put hate behind them and look toward the future. It wouldn't be easy, but things worth doing often aren't—and they were committed. They were committed to each other, to Margaret Cate, and most of all to their students. They were also committed to the community. Before the year was over, they would come to realize Hattie Cotton School was more than a building—a lot more.

Chapter Forty-One

The rest of the week following the blast at Hattie Cotton is almost a blur, especially looking at it now through a sixty-three-year-old rearview mirror. We had to report every day, but I couldn't tell you much of what we did except probably commiserate. I do remember finding out at some point our classes, Irene's and mine, would be relocated to space inside East High School. It wasn't ideal, but by that point we were just grateful to know we would have some place. I kept thinking about my students and how upset they must be. I had seen a few of them but not too many. I knew they were sad. I knew they didn't understand. I knew they wanted their school back. I also knew they would have questions, and I had better have some answers.

Although I had seen the building many times while driving by, when I found out we would be meeting at East High for the foreseeable future, I took a ride over there late in the week so I could just look at it from the outside. I remember feeling rather overwhelmed. The sheer size of it dwarfed Hattie Cotton. It was a huge building with four floors, including the basement level, which was about half below ground. The school was set back from Gallatin Pike and therefore had a large front lawn area. The façade was mostly dark red brick with lots of windows, all very plain. It almost looked like a mill building, except the middle of it was very ornate. That section appeared to be made out of gray stone and had a very Romanesque look to it. The side columns rose high, even towering over the top floor of the building. Between the two columns, at ground level, was the building's main entrance: three large evenly spaced doors with rounded tops.

I think it was Thursday or Friday when Miss Cate brought Irene and me over to East so we could check things out more closely. We needed to know a lot of really basic things, like where we would park, where we would enter and exit the building, where the kids would be able to have recess, eat lunch, and go to the bathroom. There was an entrance on the north end of the building closest to our rooms. The first trip up those three flights of stairs with Margaret taught me I needn't worry about getting in enough daily exercise. I couldn't help worrying, though, about doing it with fifty sixth graders in tow!

My room itself was...well, a storage room turned classroom. By the time we arrived for our "tour," the room was empty and clean. In fact, while we were there the janitors started moving in desks and chairs and other supplies from

Hattie Cotton. As I looked around the "room" I started thinking about how I might set things up. How I could best arrange the students' desks and mine. I took note of the light fixtures and where the windows were. I was still feeling nervous and a little sorry for myself—okay a lot sorry for myself—but, one way or another we would be ready for Monday. I was determined. So was Irene and so was Miss Cate.

Chapter Forty-Two

While Hattie Cotton's students and teachers were making preparations to get back to school, investigators were working overtime trying to find those responsible for the destruction—and hold those people accountable. On Thursday, at Nashville school's request, a restraining order was issued by Federal Judge William Miller against twelve men, including John Kasper, legally preventing them from in any way further disrupting desegregation of the city's schools.[75]

Friday saw Kasper indicted by the Davidson County Grand Jury, charged with inciting a riot. He was bound over for trial in criminal court, remaining in jail because he had been unable to raise the $2,500 bond. Local police had called in both state and federal agencies to assist in the Hattie Cotton School investigation. So far six men were being held in connection with the bombing. Investigators were running down leads, suspects were being interrogated, rewards were being offered, and local newspapers were writing scathing editorials, but so far no actual charges had been filed.[76]

In the case of Mr. Kasper, the old saying what a difference a day makes comes to mind. It would seem the southern hospitality he had enjoyed all these months was suddenly not so hospitable. It may have been because of Hattie Cotton. It may have been because Nashville did not welcome the negative national attention it was getting from the press regarding desegregation. It may have been because the racist white supremacists, or even the silent fence-sitters, finally figured out it wasn't their cause Kasper cared about, it was his cause—or causes: the notoriety, the headlines, the hero worship. Whatever the reasons, it appeared Kasper had finally worn out his welcome.

There are many public figures, though, who believe there is no such thing as "bad" publicity. John Kasper was clearly one of them. For months the northern agitator had been riding a growing swell of white frustration and resentment into a wave of successes. Consequently he had gained greater and greater name recognition. From Washington

---

[75] William Miller. Temporary Restraining Order.
[76] Egerton

to Arkansas and from Oakridge to Clinton to Nashville, the wave kept growing. On Sunday night the segregationists were riding high, their influence at its peak. But as we all know, even the mightiest, most impressive of waves, no matter their starting point, no matter their height, eventually they approach the shoreline and come crashing down.

The reality is, whether Kasper had actually placed and detonated the dynamite, or just arranged to have it done, didn't really matter. He had clearly overplayed his hand. A few days earlier he had been the hero of many white supremacists, almost a savior figure, able to play on people's fears and bigotry, convince them he could help save their way of life. By Monday night he was in jail, persona non-grata, a pariah, a leper. What a difference a day makes, indeed.

Chapter Forty-Three

One of the first things we were told was we needed to cause as little disruption to the routines of East as possible, and have as little interaction with the high school students as possible—none being the optimal. So, we designed our schedules around theirs. We would enter the building after they had started classes. We would go to and from recess when the high schoolers were in class, so as not to make hall traffic even worse and have our "little kids" bother the "big kids." And we would dismiss our students well before the high school's final bell.

Part of me wanted to decorate the room, make it homey and inviting, much like I had done at Hattie Cotton. Another part of me didn't want to get too comfortable. I was still hopeful we wouldn't have to be there all that long. In the end I really wasn't able to do too much—there just wasn't enough time. There was no large calendar hanging on the wall. I did put up a Student Work sign, but there were no bulletin boards to decorate, no cursive alphabet chart, no funny or inspirational posters. We would, however, have the most important things in any classroom, the things that make or break educational value and academic accomplishment: the students and teachers.

It dawned on me, much of what I had included in my original lesson plans would have to be revised. I would have one fairly small rolling chalkboard, so sending a group of kids to work at the board was out. There would be no filmstrips or slides, at least initially, to help make literature come alive, and few if any maps to give perspective to geography, because all of those visual aids along with the projectors had been destroyed in the blast. Basically, I realized, the only visual aid I could count on was me, along with whatever I could collect, construct, or cobble together. But those were only a few of the obstacles we needed to overcome.

We would have to find a way to have water in the room. Bathroom trips, except for emergencies, would need to be scheduled. Lunch would have to be eaten in our room. Even recess was going to be a challenge. The area we had been assigned for exercise and recess, or any outdoor activity for that matter, was between the building and the football field. It was all grass and well cared for, which was good. But there was little else good about it. The lawn sloped away from the school down to the football field. Have you ever tried to play softball or dodgeball or even whiffle-ball on a hill? With no bases? No backstop? No fence?

And we couldn't move up closer to the building where the lawn was flatter because there were classes going on with open windows. Let me say, it was not easy.

We were committed to make the best of this, because whoever's fault this nightmare was, it wasn't the students' fault. They were already paying a terrific price for someone else's horrific actions. I was determined to help ease some of their pain if there were any way possible, no matter what it took. I would have to be careful but thought surely I could find ways of using this tragedy to show we could go on. I desperately wanted my students to see and believe good things could still happen in our classroom this year, even if the classroom was a converted music department storage room. I wanted to teach them that education, whether it is academic, social, or emotional need not be, and should not be, grounded in hatred. I wanted them to understand nothing good ever comes out of hate. I would find a way.

Chapter Forty-Four

By the end of the week city hall must have been getting anxious. When a crime happens people want the criminals caught, tried, convicted, and punished. By Friday, September thirteenth, there had been a number of suspects brought in for questioning, and some were actually being held. Among them were several more of Kasper's devotees, Carroll E. Crimmins, W.D. Hodge, and William Wilkins. They had been added to the list of those taken into custody for questioning about the school bombing, after each one had been charged with vagrancy by City Court Judge Andrew Doyle and ordered to pay a $50.00 fine. This is the same Judge Doyle who told John Kasper, "You came into this town to cause racial disorder. You and others like you are responsible for any blood that may be shed. I only wish we had enough policemen to take you by the seat of your britches and the nape of your neck and throw you outside the city limits."[77] Yet, for the dynamite bombing of Hattie Cotton School, there were still no arrests.

Mayor West was not a happy man. He was proud of Nashville and its mostly law-abiding citizens. In politics, having served in Tennessee's State Senate and as Nashville's mayor, West had been instrumental in improving race relations in the city and especially in city government. He had no intention of sitting idly by and seeing those hard-won advances destroyed. He wasn't even going to allow them to be set back. Though he had to move slowly, balancing his conscience with the realities of his voter base, the mayor believed in civil rights for all. He believed in upholding the law. He believed in integration—and he was not afraid to say so. Ben West wanted answers. But so far there were none, and there were still no arrests.

Chief of Police Hosse was infuriated that this act of terrorism happened on his watch. rallied his entire department to assure teachers, students, parents, and the general public their schools would continue operating safely and smoothly. He had called in state and federal agencies, including the FBI, to assist in the investigation of the Hattie Cotton School bombing. A number of people had been detained and questioned.

---

[77] E. Thomas Wood. "Nashville Now and Then."

Detonating wires and caps had been found, both at the scene and in the trunk of a car that had been picked up. An associate of Kasper's, Charles Reed, voluntarily went to the FBI claiming he had helped Kasper hide three cases of dynamite. Reed's friend Thomas Norvell also gave a statement to the FBI claiming to know about Kasper's connection to the bombing. A restraining order was in place against ten people, including Kasper. And yet, even with all this evidence, and despite the diligence of so many local, state, and federal investigators, there were still no arrests.

A week later, school attendance numbers had steadily increased to normal or near normal levels. Demonstrations had decreased to virtually none. Twelve of the original nineteen black first-graders who began attending previously all-white schools were still doing so, seemingly with little if any controversy. Hattie Cotton School was ready to resume classes, some on campus, some off, but they would resume, nonetheless. Superintendent Bass had publicly stated he thought their "troubles were over." But the crime remained aggravating, frustrating, and unsolved. There were still no arrests.

Chapter Forty-Five

Se
eptember 17, 1957. The worst week of my life, probably the worst week
of many lives, was over. This was a new beginning. This was not going
to be the end of a nightmare, nor was it going to be "making the best of
a bad situation." No, this was going to be a brand-new beginning—the start
of something good. I would do everything I possibly could, whatever it took, to
ensure neither hatred nor destruction would define this school year.

I don't remember all the details of our first morning at East, but
somehow Irene and I, along with something like fifty students, managed to find
the right gathering place, and we trudged our way up to the top floor and our
new "room." Children being children, there was some jockeying for certain desks
and a little grumbling about "calling" certain places, but it didn't take too long
before everyone was seated. And right away the questions started. I would like
to think I remember hands going up, students waiting to be called on—I don't
think that happened, because the questions came one on top of the other: "Mrs.
Bruce, why did somebody want to blow up our school?" "Mrs. Bruce, why did
the police question my dad when he drives a bulldozer?" "When can we go back
to our school?" "What do we do for recess?" "Mrs. Bruce, why do the Negroes
want to come to our school anyway?" And so it went.

With the level of anxiety in the room, things got pretty chaotic. I knew I
was going to have to create some order and I needed to do it quickly, or I would
lose control before I could get it established. "Okay, okay," I said, somewhat
loudly. "I know you have a lot of questions—so do I—but right now, with
everybody talking at once, I can't even hear your questions, never mind respond
to them. So here's what we'll do. This morning we'll just talk. You can ask
questions, one at a time, and I'll do my best to answer them. Then, after lunch
we'll move onto other things. If you don't get everything asked this morning, we'll
talk some more this afternoon or tomorrow. Some of your questions may actually
get answered while we're doing other schoolwork anyway. But I promise, at some
point, we will get to all your questions. Deal?" They agreed, and I decided I'd
get the most difficult one out of the way first. I had to be careful, but I also had
to be honest. Kids can sense when you're lying, or just stretching the truth. They
can see it on your face and in your eyes, through your body language. They can
almost smell it, even in the sixth grade. The question needed to be answered
tactfully but honestly—for them, for me, and for Patricia Watson.

"One of you asked, 'Why do the Negroes want to come to our school anyway?' Well, obviously I am not a Negro, so I don't know if I can give you a perfectly accurate answer, but I will try my best. The first part of my answer is, we have to let Negroes go to the school nearest to where they live, because that's the law. Some people don't like the law, some people think it's a bad law, and some people think the law should never have been passed in the first place. But the fact remains, even if people don't like the law, even if they truly believe it is a bad law, it is still the law, and according to the police, the mayor, and the superintendent of schools, we have to obey the law." Not sure I was getting my point across, so I tried something else.

"Let's say Mr. Jones owns the store down the street. As much as you love to see his display of penny candy, you can't just take some without paying for it, because the law says that is stealing, and you would be breaking the law if you just took some and walked out. Or how about this: I drive in here every day from Gallatin. The law says I can't just go as fast as I want to, even if I happen to be running late some particular day—I have to obey the speed limit. It also says when I get to Lebanon I have to slow down because there are more cars and pedestrians, and drivers need to go slower and be more careful in the city limits. I have a right to drive my car, but other people have the right to be safe while I am doing so."

Still not sure I was seeing very many flickers of understanding; I tried one more example. "You know how someone gets to be mayor or governor or president, right? Yes, people vote for them, and the one who receives the most votes wins. Did you know there was a time, not so long ago, when your mothers were not allowed to vote, because the law said only men could vote? Well, after a lot of hard work by a lot of women—and some men—the United States Supreme Court passed a new law which said women over the age of twenty-one had to be allowed to vote. They said only allowing men to vote was not fair and equal for women. It is the same idea here. Do you know why you attend Hattie Cotton School? Because it's the nearest school to where you live, and the law says you have a right to go to school there. You may not have known it, because you didn't really have a reason or a need to know it, but that's why you attend Hattie Cotton. Well, the Supreme Court passed a new law making it the same for Negro children. The little Negro girl who came to Hattie Cotton on the first day of school came because it is the school closest to where she lives. Now, she didn't have to go to Hattie Cotton, but the new law said she had the right to go *there. Again, you may not have realized it, but you have always had that right. Until this new law was passed, though, she didn't." "That doesn't seem quite fair," someone remarked. "No, it doesn't, does it?"*

We had time for one more question before recess, so I decided to tackle another tough one. Someone had asked, "Why do people hate Negroes anyway?" Part of me wanted to launch into an explanation of how the question itself really demonstrated the depth of the racial disparity in our country: Why do people hate Negroes anyway? In other words, we "white people" are people and Negroes are something else. But even though it is what the question inherently implied, I knew it wasn't what she really meant, and suggesting otherwise would not be at all productive. So, I opted for an answer I thought would be helpful, and one I thought the class would understand.

"Here's the thing, all white people don't hate Negro people; some white people do, and I would bet many of those who do could not give you a concrete reason why they do. They were just raised by their parents and families not to mix or associate with Negro people. In all honesty, it goes all the way back to slavery, when Negroes were not considered to be people, just slaves, who basically existed to work plantation fields and serve their masters. Negroes, during that terrible period in our history, were considered to be property not people. I know it seems ridiculous, because obviously they are people, but that's the way things were—especially in the South where there were many cotton and tobacco plantations which needed lots of people to work the fields. So, while today, most of us have come to understand how terrible slavery was, there are still a few white people who cannot think of Negroes as people, people just like themselves, only with a different color of skin. And, since they can't think of them as people, they have come to think of them as something other than people, something lower than people. Even worse, some white people have learned to "hate" them rather than associate with them, or live beside them, or sit next to them in church, or eat near them in a restaurant."

"Mrs. Bruce," one of the kids said, "a Negro family lives right across the street from me. One of the girls is the same age as me, and we play together all the time." "I'm glad you do," I responded, "because with enough time, you and other children like you will help stop the hate."

Chapter Forty-Six

A nd so, Mrs. Bruce and her class were off to a new start in their new place. The students seemed fairly satisfied with her answers to their questions, and MaryAnne felt like she had provided them with explanations which were understandable at their level, and also truthful and reasonable enough they wouldn't anger a lot of parents; she had not forgotten the demonstrations she'd witnessed on the television news, which some of her students' parents could have attended. She had also not forgotten the wrath of the mother she'd dealt with in the principal's office at McCann the previous year.

Just before morning recess she moved on to other things. She told them where the bathrooms were and how to get there. She also said she would schedule bathroom breaks throughout the day, so they should try to go at the scheduled time and therefore minimize the number of times they had to be out in the halls and be in the way of the "big kids." They talked about recess, where it would be, and how to get there. She explained there was no lunchroom for them, so they would have to eat lunch in the classroom. They would also not have access to the library, so she said she would do her best to supply the materials and resources they might need.

By the time they were all back in the room after recess Miss Cate had arrived, and she brought with her some more of the books rescued from their room at Hattie Cotton. The janitors and some volunteers had brought over most of them when they were setting up the room, but they didn't get them all. Miss Cate had also collected as many of their personal school supplies as she could find and had placed them on a table in the room. Students who recognized their own things were allowed to pick them up. The rest were divided out among everyone else. She talked about how much she and everyone else missed them at Hattie Cotton, but she was very glad to see them and would come over as often as possible for as long as they were there. She also told them repair work had already started and she hoped it would not be too awful long before they were all back together where they belonged. In the meantime, Mrs. Bruce and Miss Spivy would be taking good care of them, and they should try hard to keep up with their schoolwork. They assured her they would and thanked her for coming and bringing their books and supplies. Then she was off to Hattie Cotton, and they pulled out their sack lunches.

When they were done eating they made a scheduled trip to the bathrooms, then lined up, single file (just in case they met anyone on the stairs), walked down the three-and-a-half flights of stairs, and out to their tilted playground. There wasn't much in the way of things to play with, but several of the girls had jump ropes and a few of the boys had balls and gloves to play catch. Honoring her word, when the kids came back in from lunch recess, she asked them for the next question, and braced herself.

Chapter Forty-Seven

Our first recess was a bit awkward—like the kids didn't quite know what to do, but it got them out of their seats, gave them a chance to run around and burn off some energy, and was a familiar part of their normal school day. Miss Cate's visit had been a nice diversion, bringing back another piece of "normal" for them. As soon as they were all back in, seated, and quiet, I asked for the next question. "Why would anyone want to blow up our school?" This was not going to be easy, and I thought hard as I considered how I would respond. Once again, I needed to answer their question honestly, but in a way they could understand and without sounding like I was blaming all white people.

"I am not sure how good of an answer I can give you, because I don't really understand myself, but I will try. There are all kinds of reasons why some people want to do bad things. They may be envious of someone and try to take what they have. They may feel like they have been cheated by someone and want to hurt them in return rather than forgive them. Or they may fear someone, fear they are going to be hurt by them in some way, and they may think the best way to protect themselves is to lash out and do the hurting first. And those are just some of the reasons people might do bad things. Another reason some people treat other people badly is just because they are different from them. For example, some people make fun of others. They may do or say mean things because the other person can't talk, or may be missing an arm or a leg, or wears glasses, or stutters, or is poor and can't wear nice clothes. Other people may treat someone badly because they are Catholic, or Jewish, or they speak Spanish or they have different colored skin, or different looking eyes. I think the biggest reason some of those people are treated badly is because we don't understand them, and people often are afraid of what they don't understand.

"In the case of our school, I think there was a combination of reasons for why someone or some group did such a terrible thing, but probably most of it was because of fear. Now I don't think anyone was afraid of one little Negro girl, but you see, black children have never gone to school with white children before. It is different, it is a big change a lot of people don't understand, and they are afraid of it. Sadly, a few of those people thought the best way to try and stop this thing they are afraid of, or think is wrong, was to try and cause as much trouble and damage as they could, even blowing up our school. I know it doesn't *seem to make sense, because it doesn't make sense to me either, but when people are afraid and they let fear control them, they often don't think clearly, and they may react or behave in very bad ways. I think this was one of those times. But I want you all to remember something else. One of the things we can do when other people do bad things is, we can show we are not bad people by doing good things."*

When I was done speaking, I still wasn't sure they totally understood, either the damage to the school or my explanation, but they seemed to at least grasp a little of what I was trying to say. It occurred to me some of them might even have been savvy enough to figure out what I was trying not to say. In any event, when I was through, one of the girls raised her hand and said, "Mrs. Bruce, isn't that kind of what Miss Cate was doing today when she brought our stuff from school, trying to do something good for us?" Hmmmm...imagine that!

Chapter Forty-Eight

While MaryAnne was busy trying to help her students adjust, she worked on staying positive. Obviously, some of their questions required difficult answers, answers which could not avoid bringing up the tragedy. But she had discovered, so long as she was careful in how her responses were framed, and sensitive as to how she directed the conversation, positive learning could result. She actually began to feel like she was making progress. Things were not so positive, though, with the investigation of the bombing.

By Monday, September 16th, the city had decided they would take no further action against John Kasper, even if he made his bond. The police and prosecutors had evidently found out he had plans to leave Nashville once he was released, and that was good enough for them. Also, within days of making their sworn statements, the voluntary confessions of Charles Reed and Thomas Norvell had been pretty much debunked. In different places and at different times the two made conflicting statements. At least one of them had been drinking the night of the alleged hiding of dynamite and several jars of gunpowder. Nothing in their statements could be verified.

Charles Reed stated he had seen the dynamite brought to his house by Kasper. Kasper had actually opened the box and Reed had seen the sticks. Norvell claimed he was out of the room when it was opened and saw only the package. Reed also claimed Kasper had asked him to keep the dynamite "to blow up a school," but he had said no. Reed went on to say he had suggested Kasper hide it in a nearby vacant house he knew of, and it was there they had hidden it.

According to Special Agent Lopez, "Norvell, in his signed statement, furnished substantially the same information as he had previously given agents orally." He stated, "Reed, however, completely changed his story." There was even discrepancy in the contents of the package which Reed said was brought to his house. Norvell did say he was at Reed's house on the night in question, and he verified Kasper's visit along with bringing "a package." However, while Reed claimed the package contained dynamite, Norvell said the "package was opened and contained literature."[78]

So, what really happened that night? Was there dynamite in the package? Did Kasper have and show Reed four jars of gunpowder? Did Reed and Kasper, "sometime prior to September 7, 1957 [ride] around Nashville surveying several schools as potential targets" as Reed claimed?[79] Were Reed and Kasper conspiring together, or was Reed just acting as an "intermediary" for Kasper, a lackey who did little more than pick up the man's mail?[80] After all, according to Special Agent Lopez, Reed was "a fifty-year-old white man with an 8th grade education with 15 or 16 admitted arrests, of low character, low mentality and doubtful morals."[81] The most we could do now is the most they could do then: speculate.

The fact is, nothing of what either man said could be corroborated, either by evidence or by a third party. Reed took FBI agents to the vacant house under which the dynamite was supposed to have been placed, but there was no evidence at all of its having been there: No powder residue, no pieces or fragments of packaging, no indentations in the ground. Even Reed admitted a lot of his story boiled down to his word against Kasper. In the end, Special Agent Lopez concluded, "Reed is either a psychopathic case or is furnishing his story motivated by the possibility of receiving a large reward, which has been offered in this matter."[82] It seems as though and would have been a more accurate conjunction in Lopez's statement.

---

[78] U.S. FBI (Sept. 13, pg. 2)
[79] Ibid (Sept. 13, pg. 2)
[80] Ibid (Sept. 13, pg. 4)
[81] Ibid Sept. 13, pg. 3)
[82] Ibid Sept. 13, pg. 1)

Chapter Forty-Nine

I really wanted to get started with something more than just answering questions about Hattie Cotton and East High, as important as they were. So, after the blow-up-our-school question, for our first class activity, I chose something even my students at McCann had enjoyed, I read to them. Thank God I had been able to rescue my Children's Literature book, an anthology which contained a number of short stories, excerpts of larger works, and poems. I wanted to lighten the mood some, so I started with one of my favorites: Gulliver's Travels.

I read for about fifteen minutes, time enough to get Gulliver introduced, somewhat characterized, and from his wrecked ship onto dry land. I took them through his deep sleep to his awakening and discovery his arms, legs, and long hair were tied to the ground. He further realized there were "several slender ligatures across [his] body, from [his] arm-pits to [his] thighs," and thus was unable to move at all. Then I stopped. Okay, I confess, I like leaving students in a little bit of suspense.

I then asked them to take out whatever they had for drawing and coloring and to draw pictures from their mind of any scene I had read about. It might be Gulliver himself, as a surgeon, or at sea, or reading. It might be his master, Mr. John Bates. It could be the scene of the shipwreck on the rock, or Gulliver waking up all tied down. They could choose whatever they wanted, but they needed to draw it and then explain it to the class. Of course, I got a few, "But Mrs. Bruce, I can't draw" complaints. I assured them, however, only effort and explanation would be graded, not artistic ability. They really did an excellent job. I had pictures of Gulliver, Gulliver with Mr. Bates, Gulliver on a ship, Gulliver in a lifeboat, and Gulliver swimming for his life, and Gulliver tied down on a beach. There were pictures of the last ship, the last ship on a rock, and some ships in crazy storms. Everyone tried their hardest (I think) and they did a fantastic job!

We still had a little time left when their drawings were done so I suggested we end the day with another question. A hand shot up and someone blurted out "How come some of the kids got to go back to our school, but we couldn't?" "Well," I began, "the part of the building damaged the most is the part where our classroom is. The way the dynamite was placed near the library, the blast damaged everything out through the east side of the building and *backwards through our wing. When I went in the building with the fireman, all the furniture in our room was pushed to the back wall, the one nearest the playground. The first and second, and third and fourth grade wings had some damage but there was little enough so that the workmen could get those sections repaired fairly quickly. Most of the damage in those areas was broken glass. Our wing was by far the worst. It wasn't just broken glass there, because all the windows were blown out, and there was damage to the walls, floors, and ceilings as well." "But they will get our room fixed sometime, right?" came the follow-up. "Absolutely!" I said, "I don't know exactly when, but they will definitely get it fixed. And think about it class, think about how difficult it would be on the first and second graders if they were the ones who had to be over here." They all agreed as much as they didn't like being where they were, it would be much harder on the little kids than on them.*

Then came the question that sort of made the day. "Mrs. Bruce," asked Thomas, "since Miss Cate did something nice for us, do you think we could do something nice for her? She must be feeling pretty sad." "I'm sure she is Thomas, and I think that's a great idea. I know Mrs. Spivy's class is writing letters to Miss Cate. Would you all like to do that as well? There was a chorus of yeses and yeahs, so we agreed we would write them the next day. The only homework I assigned that night was for them to think about what they might want to write in their letters.

We were only one day into it, but I was already beginning to think it was possible we could salvage something worthwhile out of the year. On September 10th I had been awakened to the most devastating news of my life, like something in it had died. One week later I was feeling more like something was being born. A week before I was feeling fear, dread, and immeasurable sorrow. A week later I actually had a glimmer of hope.

Chapter Fifty

The students and teachers of Hattie Cotton School weren't the only ones thinking about Miss Cate, and about trying to do something nice for her. Cards, notes, and letters were pouring in from folks all around Nashville, the State of Tennessee, and throughout the country all trying to show their support and concern for Margaret Cate and Hattie Cotton School. If Margaret didn't know how highly she was thought of before the blast, she certainly did after. All the expressions of sympathy and affection did much to ease the pain she had to have been feeling. Though it is likely Miss Cate was aching much less for herself than for her students and her school, there had to be personal grief as well, those moments when all we may have left is the ability to hope and pray. But the outpouring of public support…as you will see, was just incredible.

On September 17th, Mr. E. K. Churchwell of Churchwell's Books and Stationery in Savannah, Tennessee wrote:

> *You were just about the nicest customer we ever had. Films always came back promptly, and in good condition. Pay was always just as prompt…We had begun to feel as though the Hattie Cotton School and you were part of our business.* [83]

A parent named Williria wrote:

> *I have been thinking of you so often in the past few days…I was just sick at heart and knowing how I felt myself, I realized how much you and your faculty would need the support of your "parents" right now… Would telling you how much we love you help?…Perhaps if you could think of all the people, like us, who admire and respect you for the work you have done for us, it will help to ease the difficult days ahead.* [84]

---

[83] Margaret Cate Collection – Nashville Public Library
[84] Ibid

On the day following the bombing, Robert G. Neil of East Nashville High School wrote:

> *Dear Margaret and Teachers,*
> *My heart aches with your own. Today is no time for cowards in*
> *our schools. Stand fast; right will prevail, and may God bless and*
> *strengthen.*[85]

Ralph Wood of Abingdon Press wrote:

> *This morning during an early newscast, we heard the terrifying news*
> *that was both horrifying and sickening! There is little we can do except*
> *to extend our sympathy to the faculty, the school, and the community.*[86]

Carlene W. Collier of the Tennessee Education Association wrote:

> *It is rather difficult to say the things one would like to say to friends,*
> *when they see them going through the suffering you are now forced*
> *to do…Although there is nothing we can do, we want you to know*
> *that our thoughts are with you and you are an example of what our*
> *wonderful profession should be.*[87]

She certainly was! Those letters could go on for several more pages, so great was the love, respect, and support businesses, parents, and the academic community had for Margaret Cate and all of Hattie Cotton School. Even greater, was their need to express it. This handwritten note, just one heartfelt sentence signed by a family named Hall, captures the devotion to Hattie Cotton brilliantly: "Give us our principals and our teachers and even a rock pile and we still have the best schools." What could be added, but Amen?

---

[85] Margaret Cate Collection – Nashville Public Library
[86] Ibid
[87] Ibid

Chapter Fifty-One

I'm going to guess it might have been Thursday, after we got our stair climbing exercises done and everyone was settled, the first question I got was, "Why would the police question my daddy about the dynamiting? He's a bulldozer driver." I guess I had known the police and the FBI were investigating every angle they could think of and questioning as many people as possible with connections to the school, but it hadn't occurred to me the students' parents would be questioned. The question surprised me a little.

"Well," I began, "I don't know exactly, but I do know the police are trying as hard as they possibly can to find the people who did the bombing. They are likely trying to question anyone who they think could know something, anything, that would help in their investigation. It could be they are looking for people who might have seen something suspicious just before or around the time of the bombing, or people who maybe overheard someone talking. In the case of your daddy, since he works in construction, maybe they were hoping he had some knowledge of people having access to blasting materials. I know there was some talk in the news of dynamite having been stolen from a construction site in Franklin, Tennessee, for example. They might well have been exploring the possibility of someone knowing or hearing rumors about dynamite being missing from somewhere else. I doubt they think your daddy was involved, just trying to find out if he might know something that could help them find the people who were. Does that make sense?"

While I was talking, I remember thinking about all the ways in which I knew this would have a terrible effect on our students. I hadn't even considered this one: having their parents questioned. Yet, when you get questioned by the police about almost anything, never mind questioned by the FBI, it's hard not to feel like you are in some way being looked at as a suspect, like you're guilty of something even when you know you're not. On the other hand, if you're the police or the FBI it is your duty to do everything humanly possible to find the criminals so they can't repeat their crime. "Remember, everybody has a job to do. Miss Cate, Miss Spivy, me, we all have a job to do. We have to educate you and keep you safe while we do it. Well, the police have a job to do as well—right now, it's finding the people who blew up our school."

"Now, speaking of Miss Cate, let me pass out some paper so we can write our letters to her. When you're done, if any of you want to, you can share *yours with the rest of the class, and if we get them done in time, we can give them to her the next time she comes to visit. I know she will be really happy to get them."*

My helper of the day passed out paper, the kids got out their pencils and the writing began. Several students shared their letters with the class when they were done. I was incredibly proud of what they had written because no matter what they said, I could tell it came from their hearts. I've excerpted some of them for you:

Pat wrote:

I wanted to thank you for your hard work. I know it's been an awful strain on you...Miss Cate, I actually got tired of vacation and when this happened I was sick of vacation. Now that I've started back to school I am happier and was glad to see you again.[88]

From Billy Ray:

I would like to thank you for what you have done not only now but in the past, but I must say I think you have done a wonderful job in helping get the school fixed...[89]

Patsy wrote:

We want to thank you for the help you have done. And we are sorry things had to happen this way. We are very glad that we have a wonderful, kind person like you. We are very glad that we get to go here to school.[90]

From Dianne:

I know how you feel about our school I feel this way also. We all know what a Strain you have been under, but now that they are fixing our

---

[88] Margaret Cate Collection – Nashville Public Library
[89] Ibid
[90] Ibid

school I feel much better. The night of the explosion we all were in bed. It scared us all...[I am] happy to be in school, even with the other class.[91]

And Herbert even managed to find something positive about his makeshift classroom:

We would lick to thank you for saving our school supplies. You have don soutich a good job. I am in the six grade and hoip to be a sine panter. Our new rom ass som of the plaster of the wall and white plaster wase used then and it looks lick indian pantings.[92]

Please understand that Herbert's letter is exactly as he wrote it, but not to make him look silly or illiterate, and certainly not to make fun of him. Rather, I wanted to show how hard he tried to convey his feelings and emotions, even though writing was obviously a huge challenge for him. All of the boys and girls worked hard to let Miss Cate know just how much they cared for her and were thankful for her, and to acknowledge the pain they knew she was feeling. In her letter, Pat also said, "Miss Cate this is hard to understand but I'm trying to, but why would anyone do a thing like that because of one little child?" Out of the mouths of babes. Yes, how could anyone do a thing like that because of one little child?

---

[91] Margaret Cate Collection – Nashville Public Library
[92] Ibid

Chapter Fifty-Two

The letters MaryAnne's students wrote really were incredible. I have long said children watch the adults who actively influence their lives—and they learn from them, the good, the bad, and…the embarrassing. They learn the things we do which are good and worthy of emulation, like accepting a sincere apology, or giving someone a second chance. They also learn the things which aren't so good, like losing your cool and yelling at a student or showing favoritism. Sadly and shamefully, they were learning during all the violent demonstrations against integration as well. So many photographs of the protests leading up to the opening of school showed children participating, yelling, holding racist signs, carrying rocks or bottles. Those children were taught when you disagree with something enough, it's okay to do almost anything to express your opposition: throw rocks at people, spit on people, call people all kinds of horrible names, even blow up a school. The adults taught—and the children learned.

Those of us in education, when we're in the presence of our students, we are always teaching—always! And lest you think we aren't, consider some of what Tana had to say in her letter to Miss Cate:

Dear Miss Cate,
I would like to thank you for staying after school each day to get your work done so that in the daytime you can make your rounds of all the rooms to see how each has done.

I don't think I could thank you enough for all the times you've come around to our room and listened to the poems, because it seems like whenever you do I want to really learn the poems so you can say you're proud of all the room.[93]

See what I mean? And Tana reasoned the point even farther. Not only did Tana learn from Miss Cate when she was in her classroom, she

---

[93] Margaret Cate Collection – Nashville Public Library

learned from her when she wasn't. She learned simply from the ways Miss Cate managed her time so more of it could be spent in her students' classrooms during school hours. And the lessons didn't stop there, because they were learning from Miss Cate even when there were no classrooms. In her letter Sandra wrote, "I don't know how to show my appreciation for all you've done to get us back in school. I know it won't be long before we're back in our own classroom because you and the many others are helping." There's just no doubt about it; kids learn what they see, what they hear, and what they live. Think about the implications of that for a minute—the next time you roll through a stop sign, use a foul word, favor one student over another.

And Miss Spivy's students shared the same kinds of thoughts, ideas, and experiences as did MaryAnne's. Juanita wanted Miss Cate to know "if there is anything we can do for you, I know that Miss Spivy will be glad to let us help you. But we really do appreciate you doing all the work that you did for us." There is no doubt she meant it deeply, as did Carol, who told Miss Cate, "I appreciate what you did for our school. We are all lucky to have you for a principal." They certainly were.

The children of Hattie Cotton School, no matter their grade, were too young to have experienced such an act of ugliness, such a horrific expression of inhumanity. But we must bear witness, those actions and those actors did not carry the day. These children learned from this tragedy there were people who would not be defeated, who would not bow to or be stopped by the ugliness of bigotry, who would use the efforts at destruction to work even harder for their students. These would-be victims simply refused to be victimized, and these students would learn much as they watched their teachers and principal work for them, care for them, and love them—even more than before.

Teachers should never underestimate the influence they have with their students—and it's not possible to overestimate the responsibility that comes with it. The influence of teachers and the responsibility that accompanies it were two of the most valuable lessons MaryAnne learned during those first few days at Hattie Cotton School. They were lessons that would serve her well in the years to come.

Chapter Fifty-Three

It didn't seem quite possible, but before I knew it, Friday was here and our first four days at East were nearing an end. The week had been shortened by a day, since Monday had been Children's Day at the State Fair and they had the day off, but the week had still gone by quickly. By now everyone knew what the logistics were: how to get to the bathrooms and the playground, how to walk quietly and orderly through the halls. Miss Cate had managed to find and deliver enough textbooks, so everyone had what they needed. By Friday we were beginning to settle into something vaguely resembling a routine.

The kitchen at Hattie Cotton was back up and running, so at the beginning of our second week at East the lunch people would be bringing over bag lunches for those who normally took hot lunch—one more piece of "almost" normal. The kids really were adjusting incredibly well given the circumstances. The questions, however, continued to come, which let me know they still thought about the bombing and what it represented, and what it had done to their lives. It made sense, since they walked by the school or rode by it every day of the week—usually multiple times a day.

"Mrs. Bruce, what if they get the school fixed, and the people blow it up again?" came the question. "If that girl comes back, couldn't they just blow it up again?" "Well, Bobby," I started, "we will hope and pray it doesn't happen. Remember, the police are working very hard to try and find the men who did it. And even if they don't, they are watching all the schools carefully and will do everything they can to keep us and the buildings safe. And as far as the little girl goes, I am pretty sure she won't be back. But even if she did come back, which she has every right to do, we can't stop trying to do the right thing. If we live in fear, then the bad people win, and that would be terrible."

"Have any of you ever had to deal with a bully, either at school or at home?" I was sure some of them had, and several hands went up to confirm. "Well, bullies are able to do and say bad things because they scare whoever they are going after. And they keep coming back to do bad things because they know their victim, the person they are bullying, they know the person fears them. And as long as the person fears them, and gives in to them because of fear, the longer the bully can keep hurting them.

For example, let's say there is this boy, we'll call him Ricky. Let's say Ricky is in high school, and he plays in the band, say trumpet. Let's also say he is really good at the trumpet, and people in the band like him a lot, in part because he's so good at the trumpet. But let's also say somebody else, we'll call him Bobby, let's say Bobby plays trombone. We'll say, too, Bobby is pretty good at the trombone, but not nearly as good as Ricky is at the trumpet. Bobby doesn't like it that Ricky is more popular than he is…at least he thinks Ricky is, so Bobby is jealous of him and his abilities. Because of his jealousy, Bobby decides he's going to try and make Ricky less popular. He starts to be mean to him, calls him names and maybe shoves him a little sometimes, because he's bigger and stronger than Ricky, and he plays basketball. He is the one who is used to being popular. Bobby bullies Ricky a little more each day and Ricky is scared of him. Eventually Bobby makes Ricky's life so difficult, and Ricky is too afraid of him to say anything, he quits band so he won't have to be around Bobby anymore. Ricky loves band and is really good at it, but he quits because he fears Bobby more than he loves band. So, who wins?"

Boys and girls, remember this: Bullies only win when other people are too afraid to stand up to them. Most bullies will back down when people say, 'Stop!' loud enough and long enough. On a bigger scale, that's kind of how it is with people like the little Negro girl who went to Hattie Cotton. If we give in to the bullies, the bad people who blew up our school, if we give in to them and tell Patricia she can't come to Hattie Cotton because we're too afraid of the bullies, then who wins?"

"Mrs. Bruce," I believe Dixie said, "you told us this was only your second year being a teacher. How come you're so smart?"

I smiled and replied, "Oh Miss Dixie, thank you, but I am not 'so smart.' I just don't want to be afraid, and I don't want to give in, because I don't want the bullies to win. I want the whole Hattie Cotton community to stand up to the bullies and yell 'Stop!' as loudly as we can and for as long as it takes."

Chapter Fifty-Four

By Friday, September 20th, almost ten days had passed since the bombing, and those responsible were still at large. People were beginning to wonder if the criminals would actually get away with it. Thankfully, in the schools, things were beginning to approach "normal" again, at least by some yardsticks. Citywide attendance was back up to around ninety percent or a little better. About two-thirds of Hattie Cotton School was functioning, and the boiling waters of fierce segregationists had simmered down to tepid. John Kasper was gone, as was the activity level of most of those who drew their strength from his hateful rhetoric. They had not totally gone away, mind you, but the once mighty masses were now spreading aloe on their Kasper-induced burns under the cover of solitude. Someone once said, "the higher they climb the farther they fall." That someone was right. The only festering sore remaining was the fact no one had been arrested and charged with the bombing.

But MaryAnne was not to be consumed by it—she was concentrating totally on trying to restore feelings of safety, security, and in no small way, normalcy in the daily lives of her students. They needed to get back to reading, writing, working with fractions, identifying ecosystems, and studying geography, which were both contractual obligations and academic necessities. She worked on creating lesson plans that would be engaging, more like fun than work, but also tools for learning.

She brought in an encyclopedia from home to use in teaching geography. It didn't have a lot of pictures, but it did provide comprehensive descriptions of the countries they studied. She bought this thing called a Magnajector with her own money. It was a small machine which when set on top of the pictures or maps in a book would project them onto the wall. She was able to tie in science by drawing plants native to the various countries and labeling their parts. Then her students could extend the lesson to plants in their yards and at school.

Even more importantly than academics, though, MaryAnne's students needed to get back to feeling valued, and cared for, and loved. Those might not have been contractual or academic obligations, but to MaryAnne, they were moral and human imperatives. Fortunately, they were things at which she was exceedingly good, and which she modeled at every opportunity.

Even if something or someone needed to be criticized, she managed to be kind and upbeat about it. Whenever possible she would emphasize positives and make suggestions for improvements, rather than just highlight negatives. For Mrs. Bruce, the rewards of inspiring confidence were always better than the risks of conceding fear or indifference.

Chapter Fifty-Five

That afternoon, following lunch and recess, I continued with the next installment of Gulliver's Travels. When we left him last, Gulliver had been partially released from his bonds and given some food. From the ground, he was loaded onto some sort of skidder-like thing, with wheels attached, which author Jonathan Swift refers to as a "machine." He writes this machine was actually many such machines put together until they measured 7 feet by 4 feet, with some twenty-two wheels. Once he had been loaded onto the machine, 1,500 horses are hitched to it to pull the giant thing and convey Gulliver to the Emperor of Lilliput.

We picked up where the journey to the capitol of Lilliput began. I made sure to note any vocabulary along the way I thought they might not have previously encountered: "victuals," "countenance," "edifice," etc. I read about the emperor being brought to him upon his arrival. Rather than judge him for his incredible difference, the emperor ordered Gulliver be released from the bonds so he could stand up. The story detailed the fear the Lilliputians felt because of his enormous size, the search of his person for weapons, the emperor's order a bed be constructed for him, as well as providing him with proper sized sheets and blankets. I also highlighted the fact the emperor ordered the men who had treated the shackled prisoner badly, one nearly put out his left eye, to be bound and turned over to Gulliver for retribution. The kids were pretty impressed that rather than eat the Lilliputians or kill them with a quick toss onto the ground, Gulliver took his knife and cut the bonds of each one, and then released them.[94]

We talked about why Gulliver might have done such a thing. I reminded them Gulliver would have been smart enough to realize the sheer size of him would terrify the tiny men. They had no way of knowing what was in his heart and mind, no way of understanding he meant them no harm—not unless he found a way to show them he had no intention of doing them harm. I suggested his act of setting the men free was an act of

---

[94] Jonathan Swift. "Voyage to Lilliput."

forgiveness, and a smart way to show the Lilliputians they need not fear him, and that he did in fact care about them.

When I got done reading, I set the kids to drawing again. This time they were each to draw several pictures of what I had just read, then to write something about each picture, and finally to arrange them in story order, sort of like a "film strip" might be. I vaguely recall being able to work some math into the lesson as well, using multiplication and division to figure out what the size was of each piece of the "machine" used to transport Gulliver, and how many mattresses it would have taken to make the one for Gulliver to sleep on. It is amazing what you can do when materials are in short supply, and you have to get creative.

After the kids finished sharing their pictures, one of them said, "Mrs. Bruce, I've been thinking about what you said about Gulliver and him being able to understand why the Lilliputian people would be afraid of him, or suspicious about him because he was so different from them, 'cause he was a grown-up who could think like a grown-up. But like with us, Patricia, she's just a little girl, we can't expect her to think like that." "No, we can't," I replied. "We can't expect her to find a way to show us she means no harm, because, you're right, she's just a little girl. In our case, it's more like things are reversed—and what did we show her? I don't mean you and me, but what did some white people show her?" I've always loved it when students find ways to relate literature to life. Not a bad place to end the week.

Chapter Fifty-Six

It was not a bad place to end the week. There was still no progress in finding the criminals who destroyed the school, but there was progress in other areas. MaryAnne's students were settling into their new daily routines. They still showed signs of being upset now and then. For example, there were several more comments from kids about their parents being questioned by the police, but they didn't seem to be quite as upset about it as they had been right after the blast. Slowly but surely the kids were beginning to focus more on the here and now, as well as the future, and a little less on the past.

Miss Cate had gotten word to MaryAnne and Irene that on Monday the repaired Hattie Cotton kitchen would begin delivering lunches on the coming Monday to the kids at East. Ever the optimist, Margaret had also made a statement to the press. She specifically noted "they say the damage was $100,000 to $150,000. Not as bad as we first thought. I don't mean to minimize the problem we have. It is tremendous. But we'll make out."[95] So yes, there was progress.

To the best of our knowledge, once John Kasper made bail he got himself out of Tennessee altogether, moving on to try and spread his vitriol someplace else, unless of course every "someplace else" had the good sense to kick his sorry butt out before he had the chance to sit it anywhere. And, though Patricia Watson had not returned to Hattie Cotton, most of the other black first-graders had returned to their respective schools. There were a few parents who just could not risk the wellbeing of their children and transferred them to all-black schools, but most of them stuck it out. So, while it may not have been great progress, it was progress.

Today, it's difficult to imagine that first week of school. I keep trying to picture myself as a student there, in any of the Nashville schools, but particularly at Hattie Cotton. I have such fond memories of my early 1960s grade school. I still remember rooms, and desks, and teachers, the kitchen where we picked up our hot lunch trays and going out for recess,

---

[95] "Office Cat"

the teeter-totter and monkey bars on the playground. I still remember my mother bringing me in for my very first day of school: first grade, with Mrs. Benoit. I was excited to find a desk right next to my cousin, Kevin. Then I remember my mother asking me if I wouldn't mind moving over to a desk beside some girl who was upset and crying so I could help make her feel better. I didn't want to move, but I did. I also remember the spike heels my second-grade teacher, Mrs. Reynolds, wore, and playing Times Table Bingo with Miss Casey in the third grade. I remember we thought our fourth-grade teacher, Mrs. Langley, drank beer at lunch (we eventually discovered it was Metrecal Diet Drink). I remember trick o' treating at Mrs. Peterson's house in the fifth grade. Not only can I imagine it all—I remember all of it. What I can't imagine is the impact on me if all those memories had been blown up by a box of dynamite.

MaryAnne was determined, though. She didn't need miracles to keep her moving forward, she just needed progress, and she was seeing it. In addition to the plants they brought in from home, and the plant parts they drew in school for science, MaryAnne also brought in seed catalogs so students could learn about where these plants came from, what they needed to grow, what kinds of flowers, vegetables, or seed pods they produced. She had such good luck with the sequence drawings in her reading of Gulliver's Travels she frequently used them as part of their regular reading class as well. And in every assignment, every class task, every class discussion she found some creative, subtle way to let them know she cared about more than just their academic progress.

In every syllabus I pass out to my high school students, there is one common paragraph, no matter the grade level, no matter the course, no matter the content. It reads, "If you earn an F in this class then you will have failed the course, and that will be sad. But if you leave my room at the end of the semester not knowing that I love you and value you, then I will have failed you, and that will be tragic." MaryAnne may not have used those exact words, but she embodied them nonetheless.

Chapter Fifty-Seven

At some point fairly early on the following Monday, Miss Cate came by to visit again, both my class and Irene's. She asked the kids how they were doing and how their lessons were going. They took great delight in telling her about the troubles Gulliver was having on his travels, and in showing her their pictures and sequence drawings. She loved the various ideas for how Gulliver looked, but she especially liked their conceptions of the Lilliputians. They told her about what we were doing in arithmetic and science, and how hard it was to play on a slanted playground, but they were making the best of it and how glad they were to see her and how many times a day they had to go up and down all the stairs and…well, you get the idea.

Somebody then asked her if she knew when their classrooms might be finished so they could come back to Hattie Cotton School. Margaret said the repairs were going well and the men were working as hard and as fast as they could. Unfortunately, she added, she couldn't tell them exactly when all the work would be done, because there had been a lot of damage and therefore a lot of repair work to do. She was hopeful, however, it wouldn't be too awful long, because she missed them all and wanted them back as soon as possible.

Someone also asked her if the people who had done the bombing had been caught yet. She said as far as she knew no one had yet been arrested and charged with the bombing. A lot of people had been questioned, but sadly, the bombers had not yet been found. Still, that would not stop them from getting the damage repaired and the school back to normal. She told them the library was the part of the building with the most damage and it was taking the longest to repair, but they would definitely get it done, and it would be better than ever.

That was Margaret Cate at her best. She didn't try to ignore the evil deed nor the damage to the school. She didn't try to suggest catching the criminals was not important. But she wasn't going to dwell on the negatives nor was she going to let them. Margaret just had this way of focusing on the positives and the possibilities, as if that was the natural way things should be and would be. The kids asked her if she could stay long enough to go out for recess with them, but she said she still needed to visit with Miss Spivy's class and get back to Hattie Cotton by noontime. "But," she said, "you can be sure I will be back." As she got up to leave, I told her the whole class had written letters to her, and I put *them in her hands. She thanked them all, said how much they meant to her and she looked forward to reading every one of them. She didn't cry, but I'm pretty sure she was having to restrain herself. I also remember thinking she probably would.*

Chapter Fifty-Eight

I have always admired people who can keep their emotions in check and are able to just deal with the issue at hand and stay in the moment. I have little doubt it would have been very easy for Miss Cate to have commiserated with the students over the lack of an arrest in the bombing, for I am sure she must have felt frustrated herself. Yet, that would not have been productive in any way. It would have diverted their attention from the good things going on in their temporary classroom. It ran the risk of getting them worked up over something they could not possibly do anything about. It would have placed a mood damper over her visit with them and accomplished little if anything beyond a brief feel-sorry-for-us moment. No, wallowing in self-pity was not Margaret Cate's style.

From everything MaryAnne has said about her and from everything written about her, Margaret Cate romped in the positives of life. And on those few occasions where life handed her a pile of dung, she turned it into fertilizer. She was one of those rare individuals who had devoted her life to making the world a better place in every way she could. In September of 1957, her devotion had been severely tested, but she passed—with amazing scores.

The facts are pretty clear. Margaret Cate was loved by her family, as well as admired and respected by her church. She was an outstanding teacher, passionate about history and skilled in helping develop the same passion in her pupils. She had a way of making the students in her classroom want to learn. I was fortunate enough to speak with one of her nephews, retired Nashville attorney, George Cate, Jr. He had taken "one of Aunt Bonnie's [Margaret's] classes at East High" when he was a student there, and he spoke about how she was "able to make history come alive." "She was a great storyteller," he remarked, "as well as a great teacher, and very popular with her students."[96]   It was obvious she was as popular with her family as she was with her students and colleagues.

---

[96] George Cate-Personal Interview

Oftentimes administrators think the best teachers will make the best principals or superintendents. Such is not always the case. Sometimes those moves just create a monstrous loss for students in the classroom. But some superintendent sure knew what he was doing when he took Margaret Cate out of the classroom and made her a principal. Consider for a minute the little bit we know about her, and yet the breadth of her personality, leadership skills, and moral character she has revealed.

Remember, MaryAnne was "assigned" to her faculty. Margaret had nothing at all to do with hiring her, other than presumably agreeing to the assignment. Yet, from their first meeting she made MaryAnne feel like she would have been her first choice anyway. On August 28th, when a white adult, most likely John Kasper, came to the school to inquire about any black children who might have preregistered, she calmly and professionally replied none had. On the first day of school when Patricia Watson arrived with her mother, Margaret registered her just like she would have any other child and assigned her to a class. She braved a rowdy and vulgar crowd of men to protect and care for the child—one of her students. And even when she could have legitimately ranted or raved some, or at least gotten a little more colorful with her language, she refrained from doing so. When recalling in her affidavit the disgusting phone call she received on the early morning of September 10th, even then she maintained her usual calm and controlled dignity, only recounting "another anonymous call from a woman who expressed in rather vehement language her conviction she would not be carrying the Negro child home." Rather than cave to more stern commentary, she followed up with, "In view of the fact the school had been dynamited several hours previously, her words were quite pertinent." [97] I can only wish I would have remained as circumspect—I fear I would not.

It is difficult to imagine how different the whole nightmare might have been under the leadership of a less capable person. There can be no doubt Margaret was distraught over the destruction of her school and the devastating impact it had on the lives of so many people she loved and

---

[97] Margaret Cate

154

cared for. Yet, from the moment she arrived on the scene, perhaps even before, she focused exclusively on what was and what needed to be. There was no time to lament. No time to have a meltdown. No time to get angry or emotional. Margaret had a school to run, and it couldn't be run in the condition she found it that morning. She had a real mess on her hands, and getting angry wasn't going to clean it up. She obviously saw and realized the enormity of the task before her and, daunting or not, she started in. There were parents, police, and members of the press who wanted her time. There was a school needing to be rebuilt, a staff needing comfort and reassurance, and classes needing a place to meet. So, she picked up whatever tool she needed for the job, a pen, a phone, a broom, or a dustpan and brush. It wouldn't surprise me if at some point she even picked up a hammer or screwdriver. In a tragic few seconds the night before, the job of Hattie Cotton School's principal become exponentially more difficult and complicated. So, Margaret did the only thing she could do, the only thing she knew how—she started doing it.

Chapter Fifty-Nine

Usually we worked on arithmetic after morning recess and then on science or geography (or both) right after lunch and then ended the day with reading. Sometimes they did work in their reading books and other times I would choose something out of my Anthology of Children's Literature. In going through it the previous weekend I had found a poem by Eleanor Farjeon which I thought my students would enjoy, be able to read and understand, and hopefully find something in it to apply to their lives. Also, it was short enough I could get it all on the rolling chalkboard!

A Prayer for Little Things

Please God, take care of little things,
The fledglings that have not their wings,
Till they are big enough to fly
And stretch their wings across the sky.

And please take care of little seeds,
So small among the forest weeds,
Till they have grown as tall as trees
With leafy boughs, take care of these.

And please take care of drops of rain
Like beads upon a broken chain,
Till in some river in the sun
The many silver drops are one.

Take care of small new lambs that bleat,
Small foals that totter on their feet,
And all small creatures ever known
Till they are strong to stand alone.

And please take care of children who
Kneel down at night to pray to you,

Oh, please keep safe the little prayer
That like the big ones ask your care.[98]

 I read the poem to the class once, and then I had a couple of the students also read it aloud. Next I assigned each student a stanza, which gave me about five of them working on each one. Their job was to reread it, think about it, ask questions if they needed to, and then come up with their idea of what they thought the author was saying or suggesting. They each needed to write down their ideas and then conclude by writing a paraphrase of their stanza. I wish I could tell you exactly what each student had done with their stanza, but, alas, I cannot. I do remember, though, at least one student who had stanza five thought it talked about kids saying their bedtime prayers, and that the prayers of little kids were as important as the prayers of adults. The reason I remember that is because I remember someone else saying, "I agree, because I have been praying for Miss Cate and our school, and that little girl Patricia, and I think that's pretty important." "So do I," I responded, "so do I."

---

[98] Farjeon. "A Prayer for Little Things."

Chapter Sixty

Like her students, MaryAnne prayed regularly for Margaret and Hattie Cotton School. She prayed for the emotional health and safety of her students. She prayed for Patricia Watson, and all of the other black first-graders around the city who were braving integration. I am certain I cannot fully appreciate, really can't even partially appreciate, what those six-year-old children went through during those initial few days of the first grade. In actuality, it was probably the parents of the six-year-olds who suffered more than their children. Remember, it was the Rev. Kelly Smith, Sr. who received the threatening phone call. His six-year-old daughter, Joy, had no clue what a controversy her presence in the school was causing. I suspect most of those first-graders were pretty much like her. The parents, however, were a different story.

Children are resilient—adults not so much. Children don't have decades-long experiences of dealing with prejudice and bigotry. Racism is not innate, it is taught, and adults have had many years to learn it. Six-year-olds would not have understood the significance of sitting in certain places but not others, or only being allowed into specific bathrooms. Children just do what they are told, and unless someone calls attention to it, they don't think too much about it. Neither did they understand the concept of white schools and black schools. They just understood going to school; to them it didn't matter where. Adults? Yeah, they carried a lot more baggage, and they'd had many more years to pack the suitcases.

I am pretty sure there were a lot of activists who wanted to see integration move much more quickly, and perhaps it should have. Let's face it, had segregation not existed in the first place there would have been no schools to desegregate, and 1968 was a long way off to achieve full integration. But given the atmosphere of the day, and the horrific reaction to fewer than twenty black first graders, the stair-step plan probably made sense. With each passing year integration would become more the norm. With each passing year teachers would be able to influence and help reshape attitudes and mindsets. MaryAnne knew she couldn't rail against the evils of segregation and racial prejudice, for she did have to survive the culture of the day in order to teach. She could, however, model the golden rule of treating others the way they wanted to be treated themselves—and she did.

Whether she was teaching fractions in math, or about the people of Greece or Granada, she always found a way to connect the lesson to some other aspect of life that would feel relevant to them. For example when her students were studying rocks she worked in some of the great rock formations of the world: Stonehenge and the Rock of Gibraltar, biblical references to foundational stones and stone altars, even the characterization of Jesus as "the stone which the builders rejected."[99] Remember, she said, Jesus loved everybody. Didn't matter where they were from, what they did for work, or what color their skin was, he loved everybody, and he spoke up for everybody. The problem was some of the men in power during the time of Jesus, they were afraid of him, and so they found a way to get rid of him, to "reject him."

She also pointed out geographic areas where certain rocks were found and how they affected the local economies and architecture, like the castles of Europe, the granite of New England and the sandstone of Tennessee, which many of them had seen being mined from local quarries and being used in constructing homes and businesses right there in Nashville.

When students were learning about the solar system they made mobiles to hang from the ceiling adding more of themselves to the room. Even in *Br'er Rabbit*, one of their favorite short stories, she was able to spin a lesson. You will recall the fox and bear had tricked Br'er Rabbit into getting stuck to a "baby" they'd made out of tar, so he couldn't outrun them, and they could eat him. And of course Br'er Rabbit managed a trick of his own and was able to get himself tossed into the briar patch where the fox and bear would not go, allowing him to be free.[100] MaryAnne offered this, however: although Br'er Rabbit managed to get himself out of a tough situation, if he hadn't been so stubborn and determined to have his own way, if he'd just left Tar Baby alone and not hit him so as to get a response, there would be no tough situation for him to find a way out. Whatever assignment MaryAnne created, she tried to make it a family/life event as much as an academic lesson.

---

[99] Psalm 118:22
[100] Joel Chandler Harris. "The Wonderful Tar Baby Story."

Chapter Sixty-One

Once we got through the first full week, things began to look even more normal. We still had all those stairs to climb, the lop-sided playground to deal with, and going to the bathroom on a schedule, but we were all getting used to it. By the second week I was feeling pretty good about how we were jelling as a class. Questions had become more class focused, clarifying assignments, homework, those kinds of things, with fewer and fewer centered on the bombing. They still talked about it, but more from a standpoint of anticipating getting back than based on anger or fear. And every so often someone would still mention "that poor little girl."

Anyway, things were definitely starting to settle in, and I was feeling like a teacher again. So, I was a little surprised when, somewhere about the middle of the second week, maybe the beginning of the third, I had a mother stop by right after school, Patsy's mother, at least I think that was her name. The mother coming by didn't surprise me, but she looked a bit harried, so I immediately felt myself flush just slightly and my defenses kick in. Believe me, I still had not forgotten the mother from the year before. She asked if she could come up and talk with me, which of course I agreed to.

When we got into the room I could tell she was a bit nervous, so I asked what I could do for her. She started talking about Patsy's older sister who was getting married and how much time all the planning was taking, and how left out Patsy was feeling. She went on to say how badly the bombing and relocated classroom and affected Patsy, and then adding in all the wedding plans just made everything worse. It also meant her sister was getting ready to move out of the house, leaving Patsy as the only child for the first time. Altogether, she explained, Patsy was not handling everything very well and was acting out at home. She complained nobody cared about her and her feelings and she might as well not exist. Her mother then asked if I thought I might be able to help in any way.

Having already breathed a sigh of relief, I said I would absolutely try to find extra little ways to make Patsy feel valued and appreciated. "Oh, that would be wonderful," her mother replied. "You know," she went on, "Patsy really thinks very highly of you, she talks about you all the time, about what a great teacher you are and how kind and caring you are. If you could manage it,

I think what she would really like is to spend a weekend with you, you know, where she was sort of the center of attention. I think it might really help her...I mean if you think you could." I definitely didn't see that coming.

We talked a little more and then I told her I would speak with my husband and Miss Cate. If they had no problem, then I saw no reason why I couldn't take Patsy for a weekend. Before our conversation was over I had already begun thinking about some things we might be able to do together. It kind of sounded like it might be fun, actually. I spoke with Ralph when I got home that evening and he said it was fine with him, so I talked with Margaret the next day and she gave her okay as long as I had written permission from Patsy's mother or father. That afternoon I sent home a note with Patsy, and the next day she came in with a signed permission slip. At 3 o'clock Friday afternoon Patsy and I left Nashville headed to my home in Gallatin, talking about some of the things we might do over the weekend.

Chapter Sixty-Two

Well, let me just say the weekend was a huge success. On the way home MaryAnne made a stop at the Piggly Wiggly so she and Patsy could pick up the few things she needed for supper and breakfast the next morning. She had discovered fried chicken was one of Patsy's favorites, and fortunately it was also one of MaryAnne's specialties, thanks to the tutelage of her mother. Once they arrived home, she showed Patsy where the guest bedroom and bathroom were. Then, while Ralph and Patsy got acquainted, MaryAnne set about getting supper, which went off without a hitch.

According to MaryAnne, Patsy was a good eater, but she was even better at playing cards—a killer at Old Maid! They played several games after supper while Ralph worked on finishing his sermon for Sunday. And while they played Patsy talked. She told MaryAnne all about her sister's wedding plans and how they were going. She talked a little about her friends at school, and how sad they had all been about the bombing at Hattie Cotton, and even though where they were was better than not going to school at all, they couldn't wait to get back into their "real classroom" in their own school.

While she and Patsy were talking, MaryAnne found a way to work in some stories about getting ready for her own wedding three years or so earlier, and how difficult a lot of it had been on her younger sister. "Here I was," she said, "all excited about invitations and gifts and getting married, starting my new life, and there was my little sister, Peggy, who was left out of most of the preparations. I was thinking about starting my own family, and she was thinking about losing a big part of hers. I didn't realize it at the time, but I know now it was tough on her."

Getting along as well as they were made MaryAnne glad she had agreed for Patsy to come for the weekend and hoped she could be of some help to her, making her feel more at ease and comfortable with her life. Of course, it wasn't lost on her, either, that she was probably being as much help to Patsy's mother as she was to Patsy. She well remembered what her own mother had been through getting ready for her wedding.

By the time their conversation and card games had wound down, Patsy was exhausted and ready to say good night. The evening had gone well. Patsy seemed to be relaxed and enjoying herself, but according to MaryAnne, Patsy was not the only one who was exhausted!

Chapter Sixty-Three

The weekend really did get off to a great start. Of course, not being used to entertaining children at home for so many hours straight, I was beyond exhausted by the time I collapsed into bed. We had a good dinner, a good time playing cards, and a good conversation, but I can tell you I slept well straight through the night!

Saturday morning we all sat down to breakfast together and then Ralph had to run off to a meeting at church. I needed to do a little more grading, so Patsy sat down in front of our teeny tiny television to watch—you guessed it—Saturday morning cartoons! Have you ever tried to focus on reading student papers or grading math quizzes while the antics of Woody Woodpecker, Tom and Jerry, and Bugs Bunny's "Eh, What's up Doc?" are running in the background, dappled with the laughter of an eleven-year-old girl? It is not easy to stay on task, I'll tell you, partly for how funny the cartoons were, and partly for how funny it was listening to Patsy!

After lunch we took a ride around town so Patsy could see Gallatin. The Methodist church where Ralph was the pastor and where we'd go to Sunday school and church the next day was right next door, so she'd already seen it. I showed her the small public library in town, and we made a stop at Woolworth's Department Store. I didn't want to buy anything, but it's always fun to go "window shopping." On the way home I stopped at the Piggly Wiggly again to get the meat I needed for supper. I had asked Patsy what she would like and she said country fried steak, so country fried steak it would be.

You know, we really didn't do anything particularly special, but Patsy seemed to be enjoying herself, and it was nice getting to know each other on a different level. She talked almost nonstop, but I did get a few words in now and again. All in all we had some good conversations. Yes, I was still "the teacher," but I think it was good for her to see how outside of school, teachers live regular lives just like students do. And I know it was good for me to get to know her as someone more than "my student."

By the time we got back home Ralph was there and it was getting close to time to start supper. While I worked in the kitchen Patsy filled Ralph in on our afternoon travels. After we cleaned up from supper Ralph went to put the finishing touches on his next morning's sermon, his usual Saturday evening *routine, and Patsy and I went out on the porch to play a game of Jacks or Fiddlesticks, or it might have been Twenty Questions (honestly, I can't remember). I can remember this, though, when bedtime came, I was almost asleep on my feet.*

The next morning I fixed country ham biscuits and eggs for breakfast—no grits at our house; that was one southern dish neither of us cared for. By the time we had finished eating, cleared the table and washed the dishes, we needed to leave. It would not do for the preacher to be late for Sunday school and church.

One of the side benefits of being the preacher's wife was rarely having to cook a noon meal on Sunday. Some family almost always invited us to their house for Sunday dinner after church. It was always big and it was always good—well almost always. Usually by the time we got back home we were ready to just relax. Patsy headed for the porch with a book, and Ralph and I plopped into our chairs in the living room with the Sunday paper, and probably fell asleep! Along about 5 o'clock I am sure I got up to get supper, most likely our typical Sunday evening meal: corn bread and leftovers. After supper Ralph took us out for ice cream, one of our favorite Sunday evening things to do when the weather was nice. The shop was takeout only, and since there was no place to sit outside, we would get cones, work on them as we made our way back home, and then finish them off on our front porch.

Ours wasn't a glamorous life, because we weren't glamorous people, but it was a comfortable life. By the time Patsy and I started out for school Monday morning, it almost felt like she'd always been a part of it. Not once had she given us any trouble. She had not shown any signs of being anxious or irritable. She hadn't been moody, nor had she complained at all of being bored. She had simply come to our home, settled in, and enjoyed herself—and we had definitely enjoyed her.

Chapter Sixty-Four

By all accounts, it had been an excellent weekend in Gallatin. In fact, while MaryAnne had agreed to try and give Patsy a weekend focused on her and her wellbeing, if she were being honest, she'd say she'd gotten at least as much out of it as Patsy had. It had been a different experience for her and Ralph to consider the needs of another person, a child no less, and to be responsible for her—her comfort and safety. It was good practice for the future! It was also good for Patsy to experience the life of one of her teachers, and to hear stories about MaryAnne and her younger sister. Without a doubt, it was one of those win/win situations.

The fact is, Patsy had had such a good time she couldn't wait to get to school so she could tell all her friends about her "weekend at Mrs. Bruce's house." She rattled on and on about watching TV, what a good cook Mrs. Bruce was, going to church, going out for ice cream, and beating Mrs. Bruce at Old Maid. Of course, you don't think she was showing off do you, maybe bragging a little? Certainly no child who had just gotten something none of their other friends had would brag about it, right? Of course not.

Still, MaryAnne was happy she had agreed to take her, and even happier the weekend had gone so well. She got a chuckle out of listening to Patsy prattle on about all the things they had done and how much fun she'd had. Most everything about the weekend got embellished a little, like the "big guest bedroom" (it really wasn't big at all), and the "air-conditioned car" (it was a pretty basic Ford), but MaryAnne just took it all as a sign she really enjoyed herself.

Anyway, the day itself went well. The kids did their work, got along well on the playground, and behaved in class. And they asked lots of questions about Patsy going to her house and the things they did. MaryAnne explained Patsy's mother had given her permission, and she acknowledged, yes, they'd had a nice weekend. A few of them asked if they could go to her house some weekend, too, but it wasn't until the next day she began to wonder if Patsy's visit had been such a good idea after all. More specifically she wondered what she'd gotten herself into…

Chapter Sixty-Five

Y*ou'll never believe this, because I didn't believe it at first, either. By the time we started up to our room Tuesday morning I had twenty-three letters in my hands from parents giving their child permission to come to my house for a weekend! Of my twenty-five students, all of them except one gave me a permission slip to spend a weekend with me. Only Dixie hadn't given me one.*

Because Dixie was the only student who hadn't asked to come, I spoke with her about it. I thought maybe she was nervous to be away from home, or perhaps she wanted me to speak to her mother first. So, later in the week I asked her if she really didn't want to come or if there was some other problem I could help with. Even all these years later, I remember her answer, and the hint of sadness that went with it: "Oh no, Mrs. Bruce, it's not that I don't want to come, but my mother and I are busy on the weekends." Not quite understanding, I replied, "Well, it doesn't have to be a specific weekend; you can pick one when you're not busy." "No," she responded, "my mother and I have to entertain on the weekends." There was something in her eye and in her words telling me not to query any further. "Okay, Dixie, but if it ever works out so you can, you just let me know." And I left it at that. She was the only one who never did come.

All the other students did schedule weekends, and while it was exhausting to have kids all day during the week, and then all day and night on Saturday and Sunday, we really had a blast. It became the topic of conversation in my classroom, anytime there was space between lessons or assignments, and on the playground. They talked about what they would do, how they would do it differently than the kids from the previous weekends, what things were the most fun, what places I might take them, how nice Mr. Bruce was, what a good cook I was, and what we might eat. I had told them they could choose what they wanted for supper Friday and Saturday nights, so long as it was something I could cook. They spent a lot of time chatting amongst themselves about what so and so had eaten on their weekend and planning what they wanted. Honestly, you would have thought I was taking them to Hawaii or Disneyland instead of to my modest little home in Gallatin.

What Ralph and I had decided was I would try to pair them up. We only had one guest bedroom, so it had to be either two boys or two girls, but I am pretty sure I got everyone in before Christmas vacation. And although I was a little worried when the permissions started pouring in, those weekends at my house were probably what helped us more than any other single thing that fall to almost forget the devastation at Hattie Cotton School—and all the hate behind it. Maybe not forget it but get past it, and not let it dominate everything in the present.

Chapter Sixty-Six

As you could probably guess, the week following Patsy's visit flew by and before MaryAnne knew it Friday afternoon had arrived, and she was loading Billy Ray and Herbie into her car and setting out for Gallatin. The boys both sat in the back seat and chattered all the way. They talked about cars and their favorite baseball players and music and Elvis, and you name it. MaryAnne said hardly a word as they prattled away for the whole twenty-six-mile ride.

The boys had asked for catfish and hush puppies for supper. Once they got home and MaryAnne had shown them their room and where the bathroom was she went to the kitchen to start mixing up batter and slicing cabbage for slaw. The boys had both brought a baseball and glove, so they went out to the back yard to play catch until suppertime. By the time she called them in to wash up, both of them were famished, and she thought they would never be full. Fortunately, she'd bought way more fish than she normally did, and their appetites were satisfied before she ran out of food.

After supper was done and the dishes washed and put away, something they helped do, all four went for a walk around the neighborhood. When they got back, MaryAnne brought out a plate of Snickerdoodles and they sat on the front porch and played Jacks until dark. By the time she got the boys into bed and semi quiet, she and Ralph collapsed into their chairs in the living room, though it was not long before they collapsed into bed. The next morning breakfast was easy. Neither of the boys cared much for biscuits, so they ate corn flakes and orange juice—not as good, maybe not as nutritional, but a whole lot easier. After they ate the boys went out to play some more catch. At some point, around mid-morning, MaryAnne remembers she missed hearing their voices laughing and shouting, so she looked out toward the back yard. She got slightly nervous when she didn't see either of them, so she stepped outside to check on them. Then, when she got far enough outside to where she should have been able to see them, she got even more nervous.

The neighborhood market was on the street behind MaryAnne and Ralph's house. If you went out their front door and turned right, onto the cross street, the church was on the right. Then if you took the next right, the grocery store was on the right. So, the way it laid out, the church lot had an educational wing in the back, which was what separated the back yard of the parsonage from the back of the store, where the loading area was. By venturing around the educational wing of the church the boys had discovered the roller conveyor along the outside rear wall of the store. It was used to move boxes or bins from a delivery truck or pallet into the storage room of the market. The conveyor had rows upon rows of metal wheels that made all kinds of metallic noises when boxes were being moved along them. This one had things moving along them all right, but they weren't a couple of boxes filled with bananas, they were a couple of Coca-Cola crates filled with boys!

MaryAnne didn't get angry with the boys, actually she chuckled a bit to herself, but she did call for them to come back into her yard. Not wanting to get on the bad side of a neighbor, she also told them they really needed to go apologize to the owner of the store and then stay in her yard. The boys were disappointed, but they did as she asked. She was quite surprised, however, when they came back a few minutes later and said the man had told them he didn't mind them playing on it as long as they were careful and didn't break anything. MaryAnne said it was okay with her, as long as he didn't care, and they were careful. She did talk with the owner the next time she happened to be in the store, and he confirmed he was fine with them playing on the conveyor—he actually enjoyed seeing them have a good time and hearing them laugh.

Suffice it to say, the entire weekend went as well as it had with Patsy: fun but tiring. I probably don't have to tell you, but the roller conveyor at the market quickly became the plaything of choice from that weekend on. I probably also don't have to tell you, by Monday morning, both MaryAnne and Ralph had figured out as busy as one girl had kept them, it was a breeze compared to keeping up with two boys!

Chapter Sixty-Seven

By Sunday evening I was pretty tired, but it had been another wonderful weekend. Their energy level and the conveyor escapade notwithstanding, they were extremely good boys and we both really enjoyed having them. It wasn't anything that had been planned, not even remotely anticipated, but so far those two weekend visits had proven to be the perfect way to get to know my students on a much different level—and for them to get to know me. The extra days gave me many opportunities to help rebuild their feelings of safety and security.

Hattie Cotton School and the bombing almost always came up in conversation at some point during the weekend. I just took those times as gifts for teaching and found ways to show them we could not and should not let the bad behavior of a few bring misery to others, and our reactions to their hatred should not be more hatred. I couldn't always say as much as I wanted to, but I was able to say no matter what had been done, we would find a way to rebuild both the school and our good feelings about it and each other. I also found ways to let them know that Patricia Watson, along with the Negro children at the other schools, had done nothing wrong. The fault lay at the hands of the evil person or persons who had done the bombing.

One of the only things I was still feeling badly about was the fact I couldn't do more for Patricia and those other brave first-graders who had suffered through the turmoil so much more than the rest of us. I remember going through my Children's Lit book one evening looking for something new to teach. I found the perfect piece to illustrate the pain and heartache of racism. Not only was it about a black person, but it was also written by a black author, and there weren't many black authors in the anthology. I found it under the section titled "Call It Courage," and I want to include it here. Then you tell me if it wasn't the perfect piece for the time.

"Incident"

Once riding in old Baltimore
Heart-filled, head-filled with glee,
I saw a Baltimorean
Keep looking straight at me.

Now I was eight and very small,
And he was no whit bigger,
And so I smiled, but he poked out
His tongue, and called me, "Nigger."

I saw the whole of Baltimore
From May until December,
Of all the things that happened there
That's all that I remember.[101]

See what I mean? I wanted to read it to them. I wanted them to hear it and then read it to each other. I wanted us to talk about it—what it said and what it didn't say. I wanted us to discuss the fact of all the things the narrator saw and did in the big city of Baltimore, he only remembered that one. He might have gone to an Orioles game and seen Bob Boyd play first base. He might have gone to a movie at the Aurora Theatre, walked the waterfront, had a meal at Connolly's Sea Food House or the famous Haussner's. But of all the things he might have done, the only thing that stuck with him, the one thing he remembered, was being called a nigger. You know that old saying? It's wrong; it is so very wrong: words do hurt, sometimes they hurt worse than the sticks and stones. That's what I wanted to teach, but I just couldn't. I couldn't run the risk of angry parents or pitting parents against their kids, or against me, or possibly create one more problem for Miss Cate. I just couldn't.

---

[101] Countee Cullen. "Incident."

Chapter Sixty-Eight

There were too many times like that, when MaryAnne wanted to push further into talking to the kids about integration and racism, but she had to deal with the realities of the time and place. It did give her some satisfaction, Nashville had its bitter taste of violence, and didn't like it, even when it came to preserving a way of life. Many parents, and other white citizens as well, may still not have been ready to accept public school integration, but they were done with violence to defeat it. It wasn't a great beginning for acceptance, but it was a beginning.

As the controversy began to wane, as resistance evolved to acquiescence and then to acceptance, public conversations about segregation gave way to broader conversations about education. There seemed to be a growing recognition how and what children were being taught was ultimately more important than the color of the children in the classroom. Again, it may not have been a great beginning, and it certainly wasn't a smooth beginning, but it was a beginning.

And how did MaryAnne plug into the slowly emerging change? She just kept trying to move forward. Every day she worked hard to be the best teacher she could be, to make available the information her students needed. She designed lessons which would help them more successfully acquire knowledge and retain it, as well as to offer practical ways in which they would use it. Lessons in fractions included slices of a whole pie, squares of a whole pan of brownies, and ethnic groups of the whole US population. Literature lessons and reading aloud always involved new vocabulary and proper pronunciations, but they also included some moral lesson. Studies about the United States Constitution always included an emphasis on its application to all U.S. citizens, irrespective of where they were from, and regardless of when they became citizens. It didn't matter whether you came from Africa, Austria, or Atlanta. It didn't matter if you were white, black, or brown. If you were a U.S. citizen, then you had all the rights and privileges guaranteed by the U.S. Constitution.

One of the units in their science class focused on the planets of the solar system and the constellations most easily visible from Earth. The students drew the planets on construction paper, cut them out, and then used coat hangers to hang them from the lights. Next, she assigned a constellation to each student. The student noted where stars were, marked them with a pencil dot, and then stuck a star over each dot—those gold stars for years teachers put on A+ papers. Finally, they taped the constellations onto the wall with no windows, in approximately the same place as they would be seen in the night sky, as if the wall were overhead. The kids had a blast with the unit and also learned about how everything worked together. They discussed the fact Earth was just one tiny piece of this endless universe, and if everything didn't work together…well, you definitely didn't want to think about results. "It's not really different from all of our systems here," she told them. "If one country can't get along with other countries, we go to war, and people die. If some company pollutes a river or lake, it has a negative impact on everyone around. If one group of people can't get along with another group of people, bad things usually happen. We've all seen those results, right here in our community. But when all the stars and planets and countries and people work together, when all the systems function properly, everything operates just as it should—and life is good."

Chapter Sixty-Nine

*A*nd so went the days of the week, throughout the whole fall season. The students and I, often in concert with Irene and her class, developed a routine much like we would have had the bombing never occurred and had we never left Hattie Cotton. Somedays all the violence and protests, even the bombing, almost seemed like a distant memory, where the details have blurred and the pain dulled. The three flights of stairs and the splotchy paint were constant reminders of where we were, but the "why we were" seemed to hurt a bit less. The year was moving forward and we were going along with it. And you know what, it wasn't all bad.

Assignments continued to seem more like fun than work. I was still trying hard to design all of my lessons to both acquire new knowledge and convey some moral or real-life application, but I tried to steer those moral applications to reveal in some new way our interconnectedness as people. Sometimes I conveyed the ideas subtly, like when we talked about railroads that connected states so people and goods could be moved around the country. Other times I was more overt, like when we talked about percentages in math. They weren't too concerned about losing ten percent of their pie or even ten percent of their money, because it meant they still had ninety percent left. But they didn't like it so much when I said "Okay, let's pretend last winter's flu epidemic was catastrophic, and we lost ten percent of the US population, I mean we'd still have ninety percent left, right? So, let's think about this: for every ten of your family members one has to die—which one? It also means roughly three members of this class have to die. Who's it going to be? Which three are we going to pick?" They didn't like that at all. In school we were growing, becoming less of a classroom of individuals and more of a group.

And so, too, went the days of the weekend. It quickly got to where Ralph and I enjoyed those Friday nights to Monday mornings as much as the kids did. They could be tiring: days and nights full of cards, cartoons, and Coca Cola crates. All the trips for ice cream, to the movie theater when the dairy bar closed for the season, to Woolworth's, the grocery store, or church, those trips sometimes taxed our bodies a little. But the laughter, whether outside, in the car, or around our dining room table, fed my soul—a lot. I think somewhere in there I stopped seeing us as victims and started seeing us as survivors, maybe *even as more than survivors. We weren't just moving forward because of the calendar either, we were also growing—socially, academically, and emotionally, becoming a most interesting family.*

Looking back on what should have been the second day of classes, standing on the sidewalk and looking at the bombed-out building, I remember wondering how anything good could possibly come out of this year. Now I found myself wondering if the year would have been this good without the bombing. Don't get me wrong, I am not saying the bombing was a good thing or all of our positive experiences were worth the price we paid, but I am saying, if it had to happen, I'm glad we were able to pick up the pieces and build something strong and meaningful with them.

One of the only things still gnawing at me was Patricia Watson. We might be able to show, and therefore teach ourselves, our families, even our community it is possible to recover from tragedy. But how could we ever convey the message that what had been done to Patricia and all those other children and their families, was far worse than what had been done to us? I used every opportunity to teach kindness and dignity, to promote human value not just white value, but some part of me feared it wasn't enough. Some part of me still ached—not for me, not for Miss Cate or the building, not even for my students, but for Patricia, for her mother, for all the others who braved the wrath of so many vile people, who heard the disgusting epithets, and felt the bottles and rocks and spit and hate. I ached for them. Many days, I still do.

Chapter Seventy

As the weeks went by and fall became winter, Mrs. Bruce and her students continued to experience, learn and grow. East High wasn't where they wanted to be, but it was a whole lot better than no place. Miss Cate was faithful in her visits, for she was determined MaryAnne, Irene, and their students would not feel like they were no longer a part of Hattie Cotton School. When she came, she spent time with each class. She looked over the student's work hung on the wall. She marveled over the planet mobiles and constellations. Often, she would stay for a whole lesson so she could see and respond to what the kids were doing in the moment. And she always took time to chat briefly with each class and keep them updated on what was happening with the repairs which continued at Hattie Cotton. She clearly wanted to demonstrate they were still important members of the Hattie Cotton family, and she was still their principal.

For her part, MaryAnne shamefully exploited Margaret's efforts at maintaining her feeling of connection among her students. It was in every lesson, activity, and piece of literature she assigned. It was in every trip they took up and down the endless stairs, or to the water fountain or bathroom, when she would make up little mental games or tricks to keep them silent. It was in newspaper pictures and articles she would bring in, or the leaves and branches she'd carry over from the trees outside of Hattie Cotton. Ever present in her mind was a goal no matter what they accomplished academically, no matter the challenges a lack of supporting materials posed, the needs of her students would not be sacrificed. A building had been damaged, parts of it destroyed, but they were more than a classroom, and Hattie Cotton Elementary School was more than a building.

MaryAnne would tell you Margaret Cate amazed her. She remarked more than once if she were ever to go into administration, Margaret Cate was the kind of principal she would want to be. Margaret would probably have told you much the same thing, that MaryAnne amazed her. She knew full well what kinds of things were happening in her classroom, seeing first-hand how the students responded to them. Never once did MaryAnne complain about the three flights of stairs to be climbed every day—several times a day. She didn't complain about the lack of resources, her students not having access to a library, not even the challenging playground. She just did everything she could to offer her students the education they deserved. Miss Cate was also keenly aware of the sacrifices MaryAnne was making in her personal life for her students. She heard the kids talk about their weekends in Gallatin, the things they did, and the things Mrs. Bruce did for them. It was obvious those trips were having a huge impact on them, a very positive one. Each duo had learned to share a bedroom with his or her classmate, and the two of them had adjusted to sharing the bathroom with Mr. and Mrs. Bruce. Some had learned to help cook dinner for the very first time, while others had never been to church before. There is no telling how much those weekends helped in rebuilding a sense of community, something which had been severely damaged, both physically and emotionally. It would not surprise me if at some point that fall, Miss Cate prayerfully said a silent "thank-you" to the principal at McCann. Wouldn't surprise me at all.

Chapter Seventy-One

I don't remember what day it was, I can't even recall exactly what month it was, though I am certain it was after the first of the year. I think it was fairly soon after Christmas vacation, but it could have been later. I know Miss Cate desperately wanted us all to be back together before graduation. Obviously, we would have gone to graduation anyway, but she really wanted the entire school back under one roof so all the other students could say their formal goodbye and good luck to the sixth-graders, who would be going off to junior high school the next fall. Once the repairs were about complete, I vaguely recall going over to Hattie Cotton from East with Irene a couple of afternoons after school to get our rooms and bulletin boards and such set up, and I think our desks and supplies were moved back over on a Saturday.

What I am certain about is this: on our first day back I don't think I ever saw a happier group of students. I couldn't tell you what they were wearing; I couldn't tell you what I was wearing. As I have mentioned, sixty-plus years later, some things are still as clear as the proverbial cow bell ringing through the Swiss Alps, and some things…well, they are not. But I do remember smiles, laughter, and chatter, the sights and sounds of happy children!

Oh, it still bothered me, frankly it bothered me a lot, the authorities had never found enough evidence to charge anyone with the bombing, not Kasper, not Reed, not some Klan member. No, months later whoever had placed, set, and detonated the dynamite was still walking around free. I remained hopeful the person or persons would eventually be caught and have to answer for their crime. Yet, with every passing week, it was looking less and less likely whoever it was would ever be arrested and have to face a judge and jury.

This morning, though, I had more important things on my mind, infinitely more important. I had twenty-five happy children in my room, our room, and we were back inside of Hattie Cotton School. It was almost like the first day of school had been. I was excited and I was happy. Actually, I think I was every bit as happy as they were. We were home! My new bulletin boards were all covered and decorated. I had an oversized calendar pinned up again. My "Student Work" and "Helper of the Week" signs were back up, and around the top of the walls I had a brand new Zaner-Bloser chart. Even the gray floor tiles looked brighter.

Miss Cate had called an all-school assembly to welcome us back. She talked about what we had all been through but how determined we were and how proud she was of all of us, teachers and students alike, because of our positive attitudes and dedication to the school and to each other. She paid compliments to each teacher and to each class, and she talked about how lucky she was to be a part of such an incredible school.

There really wasn't much more I could have asked for on the first day back at Hattie Cotton. The building had been repaired and was better than ever. Irene, our students, and I had survived our temporary relocation. We no longer had stair-climbing exercises to do every time we entered or exited the building. I didn't have to schedule bathroom breaks, and no one had to go chasing balls down a hill when they got past the catcher at recess. We didn't have to be silent in the halls and we had access to a library again! I didn't even mind having to smell duplicator fluid again from our new Gestetner ditto machine. And thankfully, the protests about integration were a thing of the past. Most importantly, after all she had done for us—we had done Miss Cate proud. And yet... something was still missing...rather someone was missing...and it still bothered me...badly.

Chapter Seventy-Two

Yes, they were "home." Not only did they have a completely new room, but they also had a brand-new library with new books and encyclopedias and movie and film-strip projectors. They had a lunchroom again, where they could actually go to eat. They could go to the bathroom when they needed to! And for kids, maybe the best thing of all was having a nice, flat playground again. They were back home, and glad of it.

The return was a pretty big deal. Schools back then were much more regimented than they are today. Routines were the order of the day and strict manners, and discipline were expected and enforced. Still, Miss Cate and the other teachers had found their ways to help welcome the fifth and sixth graders back into the building. Teachers and students, all of them knew they had been missed. The students felt especially excited to have been the center of such attention during the assembly.

MaryAnne, too, was warmed by the welcome shown to them. She was also impressed with what had been done to the building during their absence. Outside there were still a few signs left from the explosion, shrubs and sections of grass which had not yet taken hold, but inside you would never have known anything had happened. The new floor tiles were waxed and buffed. The new windows were washed and completely dust free. The rebuilt library was state-of-the-art and fully stocked.

In the damaged classrooms, the buckled cement slabs had all been leveled, and then the floors were retiled. Ceilings and light fixtures had been repaired or replaced. All the walls had been patched or rebuilt as needed, and professionally repainted. There were new bulletin boards and chalkboards on the walls. Under Margaret's careful eye, everything was completed for their first day back—and it was beautiful.

As grim and hopeless as things had looked the September before, they looked a whole lot brighter now. MaryAnne was truly amazed at what Margaret, the workmen, and the janitors had been able to pull off. It seemed little short of a miracle such substantial damage had been completely repaired in a reasonably short period of time. And the best part? Everything was done and the sixth graders were back well before graduation.

Chapter Seventy-Three

Graduation was a big deal for Hattie Cotton sixth graders. It was all the talk for days, and they were truly excited. Most everyone had new clothes. Girls wore white or very light pastel colors and boys wore dress pants with white shirts and ties. My dress, which I had made, was white with a wide collar that folded back into a "V" in front and buttoned to the waist. It had a wide belt and a full gathered skirt. I wore it with white shoes with heels, something I rarely wore to school. I was as excited as they were!

Dixie, however, seemed sad. When I asked her what was going on she said she just wasn't going to graduation. I told her it wasn't something she should miss, but she responded they couldn't afford to get a dress. Dixie was small, partly, I suspect, the result of not having enough to eat and partly because her mother wanted her to watch her figure. Anyway, I had almost enough of my fabric left to make her a dress and I knew I could get the little bit more I needed. It was straight, sleeveless, and zipped up the back. I also gave her a necklace of small pink beads to wear with it. When I gave it to her a couple of days before graduation, she was as happy as I'd ever seen her. Her mother came to the ceremony—it was the only time I ever saw her. She made Dixie leave as soon as it was over so she wouldn't have to talk with anyone—but at least she came. The ceremony was followed with cookies and punch for parents and visitors. This year, perhaps more than any in the past, everyone had a wonderful time celebrating. The year started tragically but ended in triumph—at least for the most part.

The only thing still weighing on me was Patricia Watson not being with us. She obviously wouldn't have been in my class, but it troubled me greatly she had been driven away—frightened away more accurately. The other schools which had been integrated back in September seemed to be making out fine, from what anyone could tell, all of them except Hattie Cotton. The newspapers had long since stopped talking about her. Things had pretty much gotten back to normal. Yet, I couldn't help but wonder where she was and how she was doing. I wondered about her mother and how she had dealt with all the horror at the time, and if it was still bothering her. It was possible she had been able to push everything aside, just put it out of her mind, and do what she had to for Patricia. But I feared it might be one of those life-changing events which *would leave a scar, a lasting scar that never completely fades away, a constant reminder some people hated you so much they blew up a school to prevent your child from attending it. Was this one of those defining moments that makes such a profound impact it affects you for the rest of your life, the kind of catastrophic event from which you never completely recover? I wondered at times if maybe I was one of those who would never completely recover.*

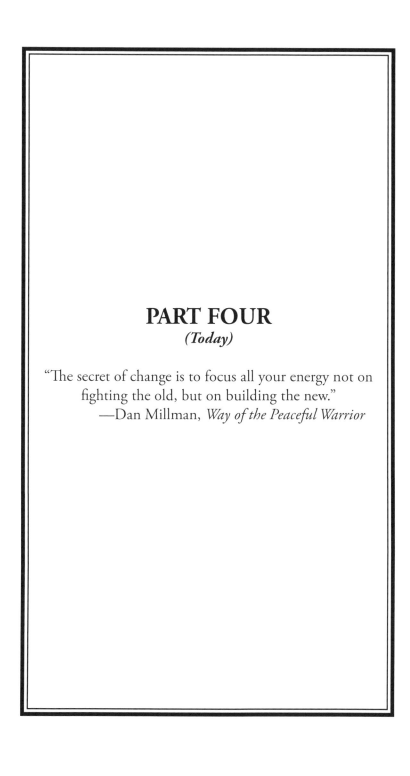

PART FOUR
(Today)

"The secret of change is to focus all your energy not on
fighting the old, but on building the new."
—Dan Millman, *Way of the Peaceful Warrior*

Today

MaryAnne Williams Bruce MacKenzie

I guess, depending on your definition of the word, in some ways MaryAnne never did "recover." The events and experiences of the 1957/58 school year had a profound impact on her. They were physically and emotionally traumatic, catastrophic actually. Yet as bitter as they were, they also had their moments of sweetness. That year at Hattie Cotton Elementary School was full of ugliness and hatred and anger and laughter and tears and smiles and determination. Some days were a mixture of fun and fear, frustration and fantasy. Others combined heartache with hope, hardship and hugs. To borrow from Dickens, that school year, at least in part, was the best of times and the worst of times. We saw some of the very worst of humanity through hate; but we also saw some of the very best of humility through love. So no, she never did recover, for her first year at Hattie Cotton School was a defining moment for MaryAnne. It altered her in ways nothing before had and nothing since could. It set the course not just of her career but of her life, determining what kind of teacher and guidance counselor she would be, as well as what kind of wife, mother, and friend she would be. How do I know these things? I've had more than forty-five years to experience them.

For MaryAnne, her career was molded and shaped largely by her first two years at Hattie Cotton School. She never really got over what the bombing did to her, her colleagues, and her students—and especially what it did to Patricia Watson. When she agreed to move to New England so her husband could attend Boston University, she insisted they not live in Boston. One of the only things MaryAnne looked forward to in moving to New Hampshire was living in a less racially divisive environment than Nashville. Ralph was assigned to pastor a church in New Hampshire. Sometime after their arrival they discovered when the church's personnel committee met to discuss the appointment, someone on the committee commented, "He's from Tennessee. You don't suppose he's a darkie do you?" Had MaryAnne known, it is highly possible they never would have left Tennessee.

The Hattie Cotton School years and desegregation had given MaryAnne a new perspective on the targets of bias and discrimination. They also gave her experience in finding unique ways to reach children. What she learned during that period would serve her well. In the early 1970s, she was investigated several times by the John Birch Society for some of her "non-traditional" and "subversive" teaching methods. MaryAnne sometimes had students sit in a circle on the floor instead of at desks. Sometimes they even sat in four-desk clusters, facing each other. She was not always at the front of the class with all attention focused on her, which undermined the authority structure. These actions would certainly qualify as subversive activities, right? One year, in order to offer additional incentive to some struggling special education students, she built a plastic "room" inside her classroom. It was made of huge sheets of heavy-duty plastic taped together, which could then be inflated with a vacuum cleaner on reverse. She filled the "room" with beanbag chairs, and the younger struggling students could go in there with their older mentor students to study. Surely she must have been a closet communist.

Those early experiences in East Nashville helped set MaryAnne up for a phenomenal career in public education. At one time or another she taught most every grade in elementary school. In the early 1970s, she earned her Master of Education followed by a Certificate of Advanced Graduate Study in counseling, after which she worked as a middle school Director of Guidance for about a decade. Following several semesters of doctoral studies in administration at Vanderbilt, MaryAnne spent the last few years of her career teaching master's level exceptional learners and special education courses in the University of New Hampshire's Education Department, as well as supervising fifth-year teacher interns. If a student needed extra help after school or before school, MaryAnne was available. If a student needed to vent, cry, or get a hug she was there for them. If an intern needed additional direction for a lesson plan or in designing their colloquium, "no problem" was the answer. You see, largely because of her experiences at Hattie Cotton School, no matter the educational level, MaryAnne's was a student-centered classroom—long before the term was ever coined.

The same giving attitude pervaded her home as well. MaryAnne has always been supportive of her husband's career. She encouraged tolerance in her children. When she knew company was coming, she always had their favorite foods ready, whether it was braised beef on rice for dinner or fresh-baked chocolate chip cookies for an afternoon snack. And more than once, in New Hampshire as in Tennessee, she would take a student home for a weekend, a child who just needed to be the center of someone's attention.

You see, even with a 1200-mile move, MaryAnne never forgot Patricia Watson or Margaret Cate or the Hattie Cotton School, nor will she ever. She understands how traumatic that one night must have been for the Watson family, because she knows how traumatic it was for her. She has grieved about it and them ever since. She doesn't hate white people, nor does she blame all of them for our racial tensions, but I can tell you, one of the biggest reasons she wanted me to write this book, to tell this story, was to perhaps, in some small way, be a part of the solution to the racism still infecting our society. This book, for her, was a way to get her story told, a story highlighting one of the greatest sins in American history, and which had tremendous national consequences, but also intensely personal connections. It was a way to share a part of her past so it might positively affect someone else's future. It was a way in which she could do now what she couldn't do then—speak the whole truth: the segregationists were wrong; the racist protesters and white supremacists were hateful; the people who set out to bomb Hattie Cotton Elementary School, they were just plain evil.

Today, MaryAnne lives with her second husband, Stephen, in Somersworth, New Hampshire. She is long since fully retired but, even at eighty-nine years old, remains very active. She still goes to the gym at least four days a week, still cooks for and entertains family and friends regularly, and loves spending time at their winter home in the Dominican Republic. She and Steve celebrated their forty-fifth anniversary in July of 2023.

Margaret Cate

Even though Margaret Cate was in the final few years of her career, I am certain those which remained were far different than they would have otherwise been. I suspect the same was true for Irene Spivy and the other Hattie Cotton teachers. Margaret made the cover of Life, as part of a feature article the magazine ran on the school bombing. While by all accounts the entire faculty of Hattie Cotton earned high marks from their students, parents, and community members, the kinds of efforts the year required were unprecedented. I doubt any of them ever again looked at public education in quite the same way. And as stated by one member of the school's PTA, Hattie Cotton had "the best school, guided by the finest principal and faculty in the U.S." No doubt the sentiment was sincere and shared by many.

When I interviewed her nephew, George Cate, I was struck by how highly he regarded Margaret, his Aunt Bonnie. He spoke of his admiration for her as his aunt, as his teacher, and as a professional. He told me she "never wavered in her dedication to public education, or in her belief integration was the right thing for America." He went on to say. "she was distressed by (the bombing), but on the other hand it did not deter her from carrying out the plan of integration." Margaret actually revealed some of the distress in a statement she made to the Nashville Scene in 1996, nearly four decades after the incident: "I'll tell you something. It was an act of terrorism that worked. While I was at Hattie Cotton, not another black child enrolled. That day brought out the best and the worst in a lot of people." There is no doubt she was correct.

It certainly brought out the best in Miss Cate. Not only did she begin arranging and coordinating repairs almost immediately, but she was there as support for her faculty as well. And although it threatened to seriously derail publication of a novel she was working on, Without a Sword, a story about the birth of Christ, was released in October of 1958. After leaving Hattie Cotton, Miss Cate served as principal of the Lockeland Elementary School before she retired. She had also served as an officer for the Middle Tennessee Teacher's Association and wrote and edited a number of stories in the children's series Jerry and Alice as well as Dick and Jane. Following a long and rich life, Margaret passed away in January of 2001. One of her obituaries began: "Margaret R. Cate, longtime Nashville educator, dies at 95; Integration advocate stood firm during '57 bombing of her school." She did indeed.

Joy Kelly Smith

I know the bombing had an enormous influence on the lives of those brave first-graders who integrated that year and, even more so, on their parents. When I interviewed Joy Kelly Smith from her home in New York City, I was amazed at the details she remembered. Even as a six-year-old in those first few days in September of 1957, she remembered what she wore on opening day; her father walking her to school for the first two weeks; the crowds that lined the streets and sidewalks as she made her way toward Clemmons School. People don't remember those kinds of details unless they represent something of great significance.

Those first few days and years were not always easy, as she had to deal with some white boys who would try to scare her and her friend as they walked home by telling their dog to "sic 'em," or the "crazy man" who would call her nigger. There were also some fellow students at school who would call her nigger or tell her she couldn't come to their birthday party, or some such thing. And Joy's mother was actually called to the school when she was in the third grade to tell her Joy would not be able to join the Brownies. Yes, you read correctly, a black girl could not become a part of the Girl Scouts. But Joy had been raised right, and she found her ways to cope. Since her father was a pastor and did not allow fighting, she decided when someone called her nigger, she would just laugh at them. Guess what? It worked!

As I was writing this section, I looked again at our Google Chat interview, which I had recorded. I am so grateful Joy was willing and able to talk with me. I sent her another message which included this question: What would you like to say to people who may have just finished reading this account of Nashville's integration, particularly to young people, black and white, who perhaps are learning for the very first time what the whole process was like? This is her response:

> *"People are people. That seems to be one of the biggest things I learned as I was going to school. Often I was the only black person or one of the few. I learned that doing things with people who look different is important, if you are open to it. There are differences and there are similarities.*

I've been with people who are uncomfortable around anyone who looks different, but I think there is much to be gained interacting with people you perceive as being different from you. I had an advantage in that my parents didn't make a big deal about me integrating a school—at least they didn't around me—so I went into it with all the expectations of a six-year-old entering the first grade. I learned things about people from experiences instead of through preconceived notions, and it has shaped my perspective on life ever since."

When Joy moved to New York City in the 1980s, one of the things she looked for was a neighborhood with diversity. She found it.[102] As a child she helped integrate our schools. Sixty odd years later she is still helping to integrate: our homes and our hearts.

Lajuanda Street Harley

For various reasons Lajuanda only stayed at Glen Elementary for the one year, but she will tell you for the most part it was a happy year, and she enjoyed it. In fact, it was almost the end of the year before she had what was essentially her only negative experience. She and one of her best friends, a white girl who lived near her, were on their way home from school, just skipping along down the street. All of a sudden the friend's older sister ran up and grabbed the girl by the back of the neck and yanked her away. Lajuanda heard her hiss, "Don't you ever go dancing down the street like that with that nigger girl." The incident upset her terribly—and she has never forgotten it.

Lajuanda Street finished school, graduated college and became a high school English teacher. She enjoyed a long and successful career in the classroom. Her mother, Sorena Street, is also a retired Nashville teacher. Both women knew the value of education, and both dedicated much of their lives trying to inspire the same sense of value in their students.

---

[102] Joy Smith

I know these things to be true because I had the pleasure and privilege of meeting Lajuanda and talking with her. MaryAnne and I met her in late May of 2021 at the Nashville Public Library, where she proudly showed us her mother's master's thesis from 1962. It was based on the success of Nashville's implementation of their desegregation plan. She credited, among other things, the support and professionalism of Nashville's administrators, elected leaders, teachers, principals, and, for the most part, parents.[103] Lajuanda also shared extensively about integration in Nashville, her role in it, and how it contributed to her growth and development, personally and professionally. She wanted to share the following:

> *"To the young people of all races and creeds: Cherish your elders. For they hold the essence of who you are and what you can become. Get as much oral history as you can for oral history is more factual than historical references because it is lived. Write it down to pass on to the coming generations for it is 'the truth—your truth.' And, as many have often quoted, 'the truth shall set you free.'"*[104]

Today, now retired from Glencliff High School, in Nashville, Tennessee, Lajuanda Street Harley lives with and helps care for her mother, who at 93 years old is one of the last living parents to have bravely helped their child take the first step on the stairway to desegregation. She is a remarkable woman with an incredible story. I am so grateful to her and for her.

School, City and State Officials

As you know, there were other children, parents, and city officials involved in desegregating Nashville's schools during the fateful period in 1957. I wish I could have talked to them all, but most are no longer with us. I do know William Bass retired at the end of the 1957/58 school year and was replaced by William Oliver. I also know they did an extraordinary job

---

[103] Sorena Street
[104] Lajuanda Harley

of guiding the Nashville School District through those tumultuous and treacherous days. I know, too, Governor Clement and Mayor Ben West did everything in their power not to just uphold the law, but to advocate for it. Both are deceased.

Frank Clement was elected governor in 1952. He was reelected in 1954 by one of the most sweeping victories in Tennessee history. He served until 1959, ran again in 1962 and won, serving another four-year term from 1963-1967. Clement was largely considered a moderate on civil rights, but the white supremacists probably branded him a traitor. He often did not take the popular position, just usually the right one. Sadly, he died in an automobile accident in 1969 at the age of forty-nine.[105]

Ben West not only guided Nashville through integration but also helped desegregate department store lunch counters and public facilities. West was known for his strong ties to Nashville's black community, which allowed him and his administration to help "improve race relations and prepare the city for the challenge of the Civil Rights movement. At one critical moment during the sit-in demonstrations of 1960, protest marchers challenged West to take a stand against segregation. He did so, and the Nashville business community quickly agreed to desegregate department store lunch counters."[106] He died on November 20, 1974.

I should also note Tennessee's U. S. Senators, **Albert Gore, Sr.** and **Estes Kefauver,** were among those in the southern delegations who refused to sign the "Southern Manifesto" which vehemently opposed the *Brown v. Board of Education* decision.

Patricia Watson

There is no doubt the bombing of Hattie Cotton School had an incredible impact on the Watson household. I know they were put into protective custody immediately after the bombing, which had to have been a shocking experience. Consider what it must have been like to believe you were the reason a school was blown up. Even if the Watsons didn't believe that the police clearly did, or they wouldn't have provided protective

---

[105] Griggs
[106] Doyle

custody after the bombing. To the best of my knowledge neither Patricia nor her mother ever spoke publicly about the bombing which altered their lives. Neither of them came forward for the 2007 Alexander Street documentary, nor for any other reunions of the integrating class of 1957.

I had tried on my own for some time to locate Patricia, not really knowing if she was even still alive. Frustrated by my lack of results, when I finally got ready to start writing, I hired a private investigator to find her, and he was successful, at least he and we thought he was. MaryAnne and I then talked at length about what might be the most respectful and least frightening way to make contact with her. We decided on an old-fashioned letter, sent through the mail. I know MaryAnne wrote the letter and sent it "Return Receipt Requested." I know it was signed for—and I know we had no response.

I hoped and prayed MaryAnne and I would have an opportunity to talk with Patricia, to hear first-hand how that horrific night affected her life, to share with her our deep sorrow. I wanted to share too, our hope this book would help raise social consciousness and awareness about the tragedy and bombing, which severely damaged a building, blew out windows for blocks around, and whose shock waves are still being felt more than sixty-five years later. I wanted desperately to invite her to be our guest of honor at the book's release, hopefully at Hattie Cotton School. But as much as we wanted to honor her, we have discovered we will have to do so through her family, for we recently learned my private investigator had the wrong Patricia Watson. Sadly, our Patricia Watson passed away in June of 2020.

We have, however, been able to speak with some of Patricia's friends and relatives and piece together small snippets of her life. Following the bombing of Hattie Cotton School, Patricia's mother withdrew her and put her into Head Elementary School in North Nashville. We also discovered the family moved around quite a bit because of her stepfather's military service, which probably explains her absence from other desegregation memorial events.

Following its rather traumatic start, Patricia's life as a young person was not always easy. She developed serious trust issues and had a difficult time learning to believe in people. Much like war veterans, she didn't talk about the bombing. Even her granddaughter didn't know about the incident and Patricia's connection to it until around the last year of her life—she just didn't talk about it.[107] Still, she was loved by and had many happy times with her favorite older cousin, Catherine, sometimes even living with her for extended periods, and Catherine says despite her inability to trust many people, if you were one of those she did let in her circle she would give you her last cent if you needed it.[108]

We know, too, Patricia was adored by her granddaughter, Lenora Watson Cassell, with whom she lived for the last several years of her life, and in whose arms she died. Lenora says of her grandmother:

> *She was hilarious and always in the mood for a party. All my friends loved her. She was the coolest most hip grandma.*[109]

So we also know she was able to overcome some of the difficulties of her younger years. Patricia came to be a loving, caring, giving adult—despite the skepticism toward and mistrust of others born during her youth. Lenora fondly recalls...

> *"If I ever needed anything from the toy I wanted as a child, to the furniture she helped me get as an adult when I was moving into my own place, she was there to help. I have a son she helped me take care of. I never had to buy groceries. One thing she loved to do the most was cook. The night she passed away she baked a cake from scratch complete with homemade icing. She cooked with love. She was my superhero."*[110]

MaryAnne and I had such high hopes of finally meeting Patricia after all these years, and harbored dreams of her being a part of this project. We are sad she won't be with us when we launch this book so she can be honored in a way she so richly deserves. Through the loving memories of her family and friends, we have tried hard to do both of those things. Rest in peace dear Patricia, and know that your life made a difference—and it still is.

---

[107] Lenora Cassell
[108] Catherine Banks
[109] Lenora Cassell
[110] Ibid

Afterword

Writing this book has been one of the greatest experiences of my life. MaryAnne and I spent many hours talking about the events she faced back in 1957, how they impacted her personally and professionally, how they influenced what took place in her myriad classrooms throughout the ensuing decades. We talked about how they in turn influenced me, again both personally and professionally. A significant part of what has made this process so poignantly rewarding was the fact even after being married for over forty-five years I learned things about her I had never known. More than once she looked at me after answering one of my many questions and said, "How is it you didn't know that?" I don't know—I guess I just never needed to know before—now I do. For example, while I had heard about Margaret Cate and the Hattie Cotton story in bits and pieces many times over the years, I had never heard the story about MaryAnne's year at McCann. I had never heard some of the details about what went on in her classroom following the bombing and her personal vow to help her students rebuild their lives. I had never heard the story about her early desires to be a missionary. How cool is it one can still learn new things about their spouse after more than four decades of marriage?

Throughout the researching, drafting, and revising of this book, I tried to put myself into MaryAnne's shoes during that sickening event, or those of Margaret Cate, or Patricia Watson, or her mother, or any of the other Hattie Cotton teachers. I've tried to imagine what it must have been like to be one of the children who integrated Nashville schools, or one of their parents. I want to understand and feel what it must have been like for them, though I doubt it's really possible. I was in Mrs. Benoit's first-grade classroom at Rollinsford Grade School in Rollinsford, New Hampshire when President Kennedy was assassinated. I was on a Danvers, Massachusetts entrance ramp to the Route 128 beltline around Boston, headed to my office in Newton, when the Challenger blew up, killing, among others, schoolteacher Christa McAuliffe, from my home state of New Hampshire. And I remember sitting with the students in my classroom at Somersworth High School on September 11, 2001 as we watched the second plane fly into the South Tower of the World Trade Center. These are all events which had a deep and lasting impact on my life. Yet all of these, for me, were things that happened to other people. As powerful an effect as they had on my life and career, how much more so would they have been if President Kennedy had been my father, Christa McAuliffe my teacher, the World Trade Center my place of employment? I am unable to imagine how overwhelmed I would have felt, how I would have continued to function.

Maybe that's why I have such a feeling of awe toward all those who endured and survived the horror of Nashville's first year of desegregation and the Hattie Cotton School bombing, of Margaret Cate, of MaryAnne and her colleagues, of Lajuanda Street Harley, Joy Kelly Smith and others, of the Hattie Cotton students, of Patricia Watson. Because even amidst a most horrible and personal tragedy, they did continue to function, they did find ways to rebuild their lives, and perhaps restore some faith in humanity. Funny, in a way, I would have these feelings of wonder and amazement and guilt all these years for a little girl I never knew. This book, for me…I think maybe it was my way of begging forgiveness.

—Steve MacKenzie

Acknowledgements

Writing this book has been a long and arduous, several-year process. It has also been an incredible learning experience, with rewards far beyond those I could have earned or deserved. Many of those rewards center on a number of people without whom none of this would have been possible. Saying thank you is not enough, but it is all I have—and it is heartfelt.

I want especially to thank Ruthie Nelson, Donna Berube, Layne Case, Joy McCauley, and Loreana Thomas for their invaluable feedback; Lajuanda Street Harley, Joy Kelly Smith and the late George Cate, for taking time to meet with me and their gracious support of this project; Betsy Phillips for her encouragement and guidance in the early stages of my work; Lenora Cassell for sharing so many precious memories of her grandmother.

I also want to thank the people in the Nashville Room and Special Archives at the Nashville Public Library for all their help, George, Bette, Phyllis, and all the folks at Premium Press America for their hard work, dedication, and diligence, but mostly for their willingness to take on me and this project.

Finally, I want to thank Principal Jocelyn Adams, Lindsay Mihalcik, Constance Hayes, and all of the faculty and staff at Hattie Cotton STEM Magnet Elementary School. Your enthusiastic support and participation in this adventure has been incredible.

To all of those listed above, and others I have surely missed, I am so grateful for the many ways you have helped bring about the completion of this book. I am humbled and forever in your debt.

Bibliography

A Child Shall Lead Them: The Desegregation of Nashville Public Schools, 1957. Anonymous Filmakers Library, 2008. https://video.alexanderstreet.com/watch/a-child-shall-lead-them-the-desegregation-of-nashville-publec-schools-1957.

Bass, W.A., Wm. Henry Oliver. "Letter for Advance Registration." Office of the Superintendent, Nashville School District. August, 1957.

"Blast Wrecks School: Hattie Cotton Plant Hit by Dynamite." The Nashville Retrospect. Vol. X, No. 3. September 2018.

Bond, Jack. "Account Of Birth Of Christ." The Nashville Banner, October 10, 1958.

California Citizen. Anonymous. Nashville Public Library

Cass, Michael. "Margaret R. Cate, longtime Nashville educator, dies at 95." The Tennessean. January 9, 2001.

Cate, Margaret. "Affidavit of Margaret Cate."

"The Closing of Prince Edward County's Schools." Virginia Museum of History & Culture. Accessed May 7, 2021. https://virginiahistory.org/learn/historical-book/chapter/closing-prince-edward-countys-schools.

Cullen, Countee. "Incident." Poem. In Anthology of Children's Literature, edited by Edna Johnson, Carrie E Scott, and Evelyn R Sickles, 2nd ed., 936. Cambridge, MA: Houghton Mifflin, 1948.

Doyle, Don H. "Ben West," Tennessee Encyclopedia. Tennessee Historical Society, March 1, 2018. http://tennesseeencyclopedia.net/entries/ben-west/.

Egerton, John. "Walking into History: The Beginning of School Desegregation in Nashville." Southern Spaces. Accessed May 7, 2021. https://southernspaces.org/2009/walking-history-beginning-school-desegregation-nashville/.

"Eisenhower and the Little Rock Crisis." Accessed May 7, 2021. http://www.americaslibrary.gov/aa/eisenhower/aa_eisenhower_littlerock_1.html.

Farjeon, Eleanor. "A Prayer for Little Things." Poem. In Anthology of Children's Literature, edited by Edna Johnson, Carrie E Scott, and Evelyn R Sickles, 2nd ed., 896. Cambridge, MA: Houghton Mifflin, 1948.

Frost, Robert. "The Road Not Taken." https://www.poetryfoundation.org/poems/44272/the-road-not-taken.

Griggs, Alan. "Frank G. Clement." Tennessee Encyclopedia. Tennessee Historical Society, March 1, 2018. http://tennesseeencyclopedia.net/entries/frank-g-clement/

Harris, Joel Chandler. "The Wonderful Tar Baby Story." Short Story. In Anthology of Children's Literature, edited by Edna Johnson, Carrie E Scott, and Evelyn R Sickles, 2nd ed., 493-4. Cambridge, MA: Houghton Mifflin, 1948.

History.com Editors. "Brown v. Board of Education." History.com. A&E Television Networks, October 27, 2009. https://www.history.com/topics/black-history/brown-v-board-of-education-of-topeka.

History.com Editors. "Emmett Till" History.com. A&E Television Networks, December 2, 2009. Updated April 20, 2021. https://www.history.com/topics/black-history/emmett-till-1

History.com Editors. "Plessy v. Ferguson." History.com. A&E Television Networks, October 29, 2009. https://www.history.com/topics/black-history/plessy-v-ferguson.

Kahn, Michael A. "Shattering the Myth about President Eisenhower's Supreme Court Appointments." Presidential Studies Quarterly 22, no. 1 (1992): 47-56. Accessed May 8, 2021. http://www.jstor.org/stable/27550903.

Kasper, John. "Segregation or Death." Faulkner at Virginia. The Virginia Spectator Jim Crow Issue. May 1957, vol. 118, no. 8, pp. 21. 34-37. Media. Accessed May 7, 2021. https://faulkner.lib.virginia.edu/media%3Fid=spectator12.html.

Mason, Chester. "An Open Letter To All Nashville Parents." Parents Preference Committee. Nashville Public Library. 1957.

Miller, William E. United States District Court, Middle District of Tennessee, Nashville Division. Civil Action No. 2094. Temporary Restraining Order. September 12, 1957.

"The New Colossus." National Parks Service. U.S. Department of the Interior. Accessed May 7, 2021. https://www.nps.gov/stli/learn/historyculture/colossus.htm#:~:text=%22Give%20me%20your%20tired%2C%20your,refuse%20of%20your%20teeming%20shore.

"New School To Honor Memory of Beloved Teacher." The Nashville Room. Nashville Public Library.

"Office Cat." Kentucky New Era. Formerly Hopkinsville New Era. September 1957.

"Racism." Accessed June 15, 2021. https://www.usnews.com/topics/subjects/racism.

"The Southern Manifesto," n.d. https://faculty.washington.edu/joyann/STEPspring2007/Southern_Manifesto.doc.

Street, Sorena Roberta Lee. Partial Desegregation of Nashville City Public Schools. Thesis. Graduate School of Tennessee Agricultural and Industrial State University. August 1962.

Swift, Jonathan. "Voyage to Lilliput." Short Story. In Anthology of Children's Literature, edited by Edna Johnson, Carrie E Scott, and Evelyn R Sickles, 2nd ed., 509–16. Cambridge, MA: Houghton Mifflin, 1948.

Tennessee Federation for Constitutional Government. Special Newsletter to Members. October, 1955. file:///C:/Users/Admin/Downloads/p16877coll8_225%20(2).pdf.

U.S. Federal Bureau of Investigation, Office Memorandum: to the Attorney General regarding the Hattie Cotton School Bombing. September 13, 1957. file:///C:/Users/Admin/Documents/Miss%20Cate/FBI%20files%20RD-57111-44-HQ-12298-Secion-1-Serial-1-47-Box-595%20(1).pdf.

"'We Kept the Discussion at an Adult Level': Jack Kershaw and the Tennessee Federation for Constitutional Government." Southern Cultures, January 22, 2021. https://www.southerncultures.org/article/we-kept-the-discussion-at-an-adult-level-jack-kershaw-and-the-tennessee-federation-for-constitutional-government/.

Wood, E. Thomas. "Nashville Now and Then: An Explosive Moment. NashvillePost. September 7, 2007.

Wynn, Linda T. "Kelly v. Board of Education: The Beginning of School Desegregation in Nashville." Profiles of African Americans in Tennessee. https://www.tnstate.edu/library/documents/KellyvBdofEduc.pdf

Made in the USA
Columbia, SC
20 May 2024

35924360R00124